P9-CCC-331

# Life Is Worth Living

## *Books by Bishop Sheen*

GOD AND INTELLIGENCE
RELIGION WITHOUT GOD
THE LIFE OF ALL LIVING
THE DIVINE ROMANCE
OLD ERRORS AND NEW LABELS
MOODS AND TRUTHS
THE WAY OF THE CROSS
THE SEVEN LAST WORDS
THE ETERNAL GALILEAN
THE PHILOSOPHY OF SCIENCE
THE MYSTICAL BODY OF CHRIST
CALVARY AND THE MASS
THE MORAL UNIVERSE
THE CROSS AND THE BEATITUDES
THE CROSS AND THE CRISIS
LIBERTY, EQUALITY AND FRATERNITY
THE RAINBOW OF SORROW
VICTORY OVER VICE
WHENCE COME WARS
THE SEVEN VIRTUES
FOR GOD AND COUNTRY
A DECLARATION OF DEPENDENCE
GOD AND WAR
THE DIVINE VERDICT
THE ARMOR OF GOD
PHILOSOPHIES AT WAR
SEVEN WORDS TO THE CROSS
SEVEN PILLARS OF PEACE
LOVE ONE ANOTHER
FREEDOM UNDER GOD
COMMUNISM AND THE CONSCIENCE OF THE WEST
THE PHILOSOPHY OF RELIGION
PEACE OF SOUL
LIFT UP YOUR HEART
THREE TO GET MARRIED
THE WORLD'S FIRST LOVE
WAY TO HAPPINESS
LIFE IS WORTH LIVING

# Life Is Worth Living

BY

THE MOST REVEREND

Fulton J. Sheen, D.D.

*Agrégé en Philosophie de L'Université de Louvain*
*Auxiliary Bishop of New York*
*National Director, World Mission Society for the Propagation of the Faith*

ILLUSTRATIONS BY DIK BROWNE

McGraw-Hill Book Company, Inc.

NEW YORK TORONTO LONDON

LIFE IS WORTH LIVING



*Library of Congress Catalog Card Number: 53-11650*

Nihil obstat:
John M. A. Fearns, S.T.D., Censor Librorum

Imprimatur:
Francis Cardinal Spellman, Archbishop of New York
New York: Sept. 5, 1953

The nihil obstat and imprimatur are official declarations that a book or pamphlet is free of doctrinal or moral error. No implication is contained therein that those who have granted the nihil obstat and imprimatur agree with the contents, opinions, or statements expressed.

Published by the McGraw-Hill Book Company, Inc.
Printed in the United States of America
*First printing 150,000 October, 1953*

DEDICATED

TO

OUR HEAVENLY MOTHER

WHO

STANDS BEHIND ME

AT

EVERY TELECAST

AND

BEFORE WHOM I KNEEL

IN FILIAL LOVE

THAT THESE WORDS

BORNE ON WAVES OF LIGHT

MAY BRING

READERS TO THE WORD

AND

THE LIGHT OF THE WORLD

# Preface

Let it never be said again that it is difficult to write a book. It is now proven that if a person talks only half an hour a week for twenty-six weeks, he already has enough material for a book. That is how this book was written.

Our telecasts were given without notes of any kind, nor were they written out prior to appearing before the camera. But inasmuch as the telecasts were recorded on film, all that was necessary was to transcribe them into a book. Though the ideas and the words are the same as the telecasts, there has been one substantial change. The author, while willing to have his words recorded in print, was reluctant to perpetuate his abominable drawings on the blackboard. In deference to the good taste of the readers, he asked his friend Dik Browne to re-do the drawings in such a way as to contain substantially the original ideas. As Alice in Wonderland said: "What is the use of a book without pictures or conversations?"

The request of the audience for transcriptions of the telecasts is not a tribute to the author, but to the listeners. The American public, in addition to pleasant diversion and good humor done so excellently on some programs, and in addition to the isolated bits of information communicated so skillfully on other programs, has long yearned for a reasoned presentation of a serious idea, to fill up the void of hearts and the yearning of minds for a pattern and a way of life. The supplying of a want of this kind is not due to the skill of the one who presents the ideas; it is due rather to the audience who wanted them in the first place. He who distributes bread to hungry people must not flatter himself that his cooking is good; let him not forget that the people already have an appetite. As wise old Socrates said: "The best flavoring for drink is thirst." It is ardently to be hoped that others will also supply the spiritual, moral, and intellectual demands of the American people, to the end that they may be unified by that *Pietas* which embraces love of God, love of neighbor, and love of country.

On television, as well as in the arts and the sciences, he who appears before the public may well ask himself: "What powers hast thou, that did not come to thee by gift? And if they came to thee by gift, why dost thou boast of them, as if there were no gift in question?" The talents of singing, painting, talking, teaching, are all gifts of God. No praise therefore is due to the author of these telecasts. If there be gratitude for putting them in print, the author accepts it as the window receives light, namely, to pass thanks back again to God, the Author of all good gifts. However, the imperfections, the failings, and the marring of the gifts are due to the window itself.

In this spirit we offer these telecasts to the public, in the fervent hope that they may draw at least one soul closer to God; if they do that, the author will feel he is fulfilling in a small way the vocation to which the Good Lord has called him.

# Contents

# Life Is Worth Living

CHAPTER ONE

# Life Is Worth Living?

Is life worth living, or is it dull and monotonous? Life *is* monotonous if it is meaningless; it is *not* monotonous if it has a purpose.

The prospect of seeing the same program on television for a number of weeks is this problem in minor form. Will not repetition of the same format, the same personality, the same chalk, the same blackboard, and the same angel create monotony? Repetition does generally beget boredom. However, two beautiful compensations have been given a television audience to avoid such boredom: one is a dial, the other is a wrist. Put both together and all the forces of science and advertising vanish into nothingness.

Life is monotonous if it has no goal or purpose. When we do not know why we are here or where we are going, then life is full of frustrations and unhappiness. When there is no goal or over-all purpose, people generally concentrate on motion. Instead of working toward an ideal, they keep changing the ideal and calling it "progress." They do not know where they are going, but they are certainly "on their way." Life is then like a radio in the early days. Remember? No one seemed to be interested in getting a particular program. He was interested only in picking up distant places, sitting up all night, turning the dial. The next morning he would say with glee, "You know, at three o'clock last night I got Washington, then Mobile, and I even heard Peoria."

Those who have no ultimate destiny for life really can never say they are making progress; if there is no fixed point, they can never say whether they are getting to their goal or not. Life under these circumstances is boring. A sculptor after hacking and cutting away at a block of marble all day was asked, "What are you making?"

He said, "I really don't know. I haven't seen the plans."

People live ten, twenty, thirty, fifty years without a plan. No wonder they find their existence humdrum and tiresome. If they were farmers, they would probably plant wheat one week, root it up and plant barley the next; then dig up the barley and plant watermelon; then dig up the watermelon another week and plant oats. Fall comes around and they have no harvest; if they repeated that process for years, they could go crazy. It is the meaninglessness of life that makes it wearisome.

Some change their philosophy of life with every book they read: one book sells them on Freud, the next on Marx; materialists one year, idealists the next; cynics for another period, and liberals for still another. They have their quivers full of arrows, but no fixed target. As no game makes the hunter tired of the sport, so the want of destiny makes the mind bored with life.

Boredom can lead to revolution. A boy is given a BB gun. If the father gives him a target, for example, a bull's-eye on the side of a barn or an old tin can, the boy is happy to shoot at it, and use his gun as it ought to be used. As soon as the target is rejected or ignored or not given, generally he goes in for shooting anything, particularly school windows. The revolutionary spirit in the world today is born of such purposeless and meaningless existence.

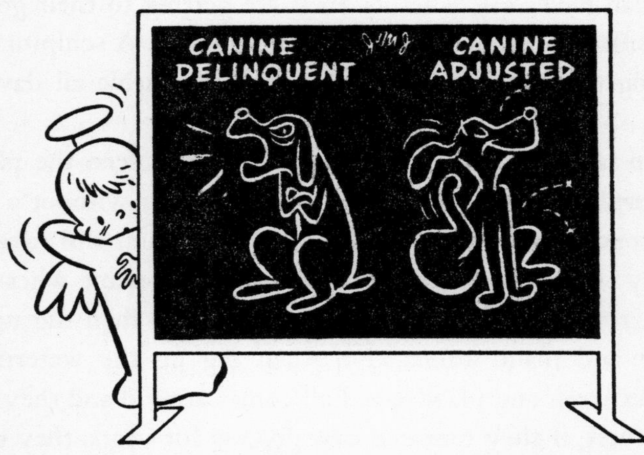


A university kept dogs for experimental purposes in two separate cages. In one cage were dogs without fleas; in the other were dogs with fleas who were waiting to be dipped and "defleaed." The professors noted that the dogs with fleas were more tranquil than the dogs without fleas, because they had something to keep them busy. The others howled and barked and in general created many problems of canine delinquency. The scientists concluded that physiological economy is directed to work and the expenditure of energy. The restlessness of the flealess dogs was a kind of regulatory mechanism for keeping the organism fit. In the higher realms, man's powers are directed to the expenditure of energy for an over-all purpose; if he lacks it, his giddiness and restlessness and consequent boredom are the price he has to pay. The most bored people in life are not the underprivileged but the overprivileged. The moral is not to have "fleas" or annoyances and troubles; but the moral is to have something to *do* and *live for*, not for today and tomorrow, but *always*.

When life has no intentional destiny; when it has no bivouac, no harbor, no ideal, it is full of mediocrity and tedium. It then becomes completely exteriorized with consequent loss of much power and peace.

As Stephen Vincent Benét put it:

> Life is not lost by dying; Life is lost
> Minute by minute, day by dragging day,
> In all the thousand small uncaring ways.

Where there are no inner resources, but only staleness and flatness, such people say life has frustrated them: *No! They have frustrated life*. They excuse themselves saying they are bored because they are not loved: No! They are bored because they do not love; because they have denied love.

(Incidentally, just as soon as I began to quote that poem the camera moved toward me like an enemy tank. The one moment one must concentrate is when poetry is recited. Why camera men want close-ups in poetical moments is not for me to divine. I must just remember to be prepared in subsequent programs. That Cyclops' eye, Camera No. 2, can be the most distracting thing in television.)

Thus far we have considered one alternative: Life does not seem worth living if it has no goal or purpose. On the other hand, life is thrilling if it has a destiny.

What we call the ultimate purpose of life is one beyond all immediate or proximate goals, such as a man wanting to become a farmer, or a woman wanting to become a nurse. The purpose that survives when these lesser goals have been achieved, is the ultimate goal. No one can have two final purposes in life any more than he can walk to the right and left at the same time. The final purpose is, therefore, unique—the grand powerhouse whence flows the current for all the particular tasks of living.

The best way to discover it is to study the nature of man. We are to some extent like the rest of creation. For example, we have existence, or being, like stones, oxygen, and sand. But man also has life, which makes him like flowers and trees, which vegetate and grow and reproduce. Man also has senses like the animal, by which he enters into contact with the great external environment, from stars to the food which lies at his finger tips. But man has something unique; he is not just the sum of all of these. What man has peculiar unto himself is the fact that man is a *thinking* and a *willing* being. First of all, he can think thoughts that surpass the knowledge of the senses, *e.g.*, causes, the beautiful, or the relatedness between things. But he also has freedom. He can choose, decide, and determine his targets both near and far.

This superior intellect and will of man wants many things, such as to make money, to be the head of a labor union (though the two are not mutually exclusive), to marry the boss's daughter, etc. But what he basically wants in common with all other humans, is happiness. This happiness obviously does not revolve around external things, such as a big income without income tax, for such things are *external* to him. He wants to be happy on the *inside*.

Man wants three things: life, knowledge, and love.

The *life* he wants is not a life for two more minutes, but the fullness of life without wrinkles, worry, or old age. The *truth* he wants is not only the knowledge of geography to the exclusion of literature or the truths of science to the exclusion of philosophy; he wants to know all things. Man is incurably curious.

Finally, he wants *love*. He needs it because he is incomplete within himself. He wants a love without jealousy, without hate, and above all, a love without satiety—a love with a constant ecstasy in which there is neither loneliness nor boredom.

Man does not find that enduring life, that all-embracing knowledge, that joyful love here below. Here he finds life is mingled with death; truth with error; love with hate.

He knows he would not be craving for such happiness, if it did not exist. He would not have eyes if there were no light or things to see. If there is the fraction, there ought to be the whole. His search then becomes like looking for the source of light in this theater. It is not under this blackboard, for here light is mingled with darkness; it is not under the camera, for there light is mingled with shadow. If we are to discover the source of light in this theater, we have to go out to this bright light shining above us. In like manner, if we are to find the source of the life, truth, and love that is in the world, we have to go to a Life that is not mingled with its shadow, death; to a Truth that is not mingled with its shadow, error; to a Love that is not mingled with its shadow, hate. We must go out to Pure Life, Pure Truth, Pure Love, and that is the definition of God. He is the ultimate goal of life; from Him we came, and in Him alone do we find our peace.

Many think, when we say that man's ultimate happiness is union with God, that God is to be conceived as something extrinsic to man, as a kind of a pious "extra," or that He is related to us as a reward for a good life, or as a medal is related to study. A gold medal at the end of the school year is not intrinsically related to study. Many do excellent work in school and get no medals. God and the happiness of Heaven are not related to us that way. Rather God and Heaven are related to one another as blooming to a rose, or as a peach to a peach tree, or as an acorn to an oak, namely, as our intrinsic perfection without which we are incomplete, and with which we are happy.

Over my head is a microphone. You cannot see it on your television. That microphone is at the end of a long iron pole and is actually only about eight inches above my head. I always admire the restraint of the boom man. He must be tempted a thousand times a night to hit a poor performer over the head with it. All he would have to do would be to let it drop. As he could hit an actor on the "bean," he could hit a Bishop on the "beanie." If the microphone were endowed with consciousness and we asked it, "When are you happy?" the microphone would say, "When I pick up sound."

"Are you happy when you hit a Bishop on the 'beanie?' "

"Only as an amusing distraction."

When are we most happy? When we do that for which we are made, as the microphone is happy when it does that for which it was made. Then there is a thrill and a romance to life.

It may be objected that there are people who are full of life who hate repetition; therefore, working toward the ideal goal is boring. No! Look at those who are full of life; they love repetition. Put a child on your knees and bounce it up and down two or three times; the child will say, "Do it again."

If you tell a child a funny story—I can remember my grandmother telling me the story of an Indian who came to kill a farmer who was splitting logs. The farmer induced the Indian to put his fingers in the split log for a second, which he did and was held prisoner. I never found out what happened to either the farmer or the Indian, but I said to her at least a thousand times, "Tell me again." The child never says, "That's an old story; I heard Uncle Ed tell it last week." He says, "Tell me again." You blow smoke through your nose or you blow it through your ears, as I once thought an uncle could do, and the child will say, "Do it again."

When Divine Life came to this earth, He reechoed the lesson of the Thrill of Monotony. St. Peter asked how many times we should forgive. Peter thought seven times was enough. Our Lord said, "seventy times seven." There were three sweet monotonies in His Life—thirty years obeying, three years teaching, three hours redeeming. He passed on to us the thrill of being born again, which was made a condition for entering into the Kingdom of Heaven.

Because God is full of life, I imagine each morning Almighty God says to the sun, "Do it again"; and every evening to the moon and the stars, "Do it again"; and every springtime to the daisies, "Do it again"; and every time a child is born into the world asking for a curtain call, that the heart of the God might once more ring out in the heart of the babe.

Life is full of romance and thrill when it has one over-all purpose, namely, to be one with a Life that is Personal enough to be a Father; one with a Truth that is Personal enough to be the Wisdom from whence come all Art and Science; and one that is Personal enough to be a Love that is a "Passionless Passion, a wild Tranquility."

Life is Worth Living when we live each day to become closer to God. When you have said your prayers, offered your actions in union with God, continue to enjoy the "Thrill of Monotony," and *Do it again!*

CHAPTER TWO

# War As a Judgment of God

I see you are back to have your faith lifted!

Many inquirers wanted to know how we could finish a telecast without any notes on a precise second. There are two principles to be kept in mind to achieve this. One is to remember that there are always two parts to a speech: the beginning and the end. The aim is to bring them as closely together as possible. The other principle is to conclude. One tries to decide the idea with which he will conclude; then one sets aside for it a certain time period, such as two minutes or three minutes and fifteen seconds. You look at the clock until you have that much time left, swing into the conclusion, and then at the appointed time you stop speaking.

Our subject is war. First of all, a word about the frequency of wars or the history of wars. Some years ago a learned professor of Brussels studied all the wars from 1496 B.C. to 1861 A.D. That was equivalent to 3,357 years of history. Out of those 3,357 years, how many years of war do you suppose there were? 3,130 years of war! Or only 227 years of peace. The ratio of war to peace was over fourteen years of war for every one year of peace.

Another interesting fact is the rapidity of war in modern times. The interval is becoming closer and closer between wars. The interval between the Napoleonic and the Franco-Prussian Wars was fifty-five years. The interval between the Franco-Prussian War and World War I was forty-three years. The interval between World War I and World War II was twenty-one years. Fifty-five, forty-three, twenty-one—this at a time when man was supposed to have all the material conditions essential for his happiness. And now we live under the threat of cosmic suicide.

Now, consider the problem of the machinery of peace to stop war. Consider the treaties of peace that were made by the League of Nations between 1920 and 1939, the year of the outbreak of World War II. In nineteen years, 4,568 treaties of peace were signed! In the eleven months preceding the outbreak of World War II, 211 treaties of peace were signed. Were these treaties of peace written on paper, or were they written in the hearts of men? And we must ask ourselves as we hear of treaties being written today, whether the treaties of the UN are written with the full cognizance of the fact that those who sign them are responsible before God? Nations signing such treaties are often like husband and wife who call one another "dearie" when out to a cocktail party, and "brute" in their own home. There may be some justification for those who ask whether modern peace is nothing but an interval between wars?

Next let us investigate the causes of war.

There are actually two causes of war, the *external* and the *internal.* The external causes of war, according to William Penn, are three: to keep, to add, and to recover.

Of the internal causes of war, St. James gives the best explanation.

> What leads to war, what leads to quarrelling among you?
> I will tell you what leads to them;
> The appetites which infest your mortal bodies.

Wars come from egotism and selfishness. Every macrocosmic or world war has its origin in microcosmic wars going on inside of millions and millions of individuals.

Maybe this illustration will help us.

Here is a man. His name is "Two Star" Hennessey. To indicate that he has a conflict going on inside of him, the eyebrows are arrows, which are directed against one another; he is a kind of divided personality. The civil war on the inside is between what he thinks he is, and what he actually is, between the way God made him, and the way he made himself, between the moral law that *ought* to govern his life, and the selfishness that actually determines his actions. When civil wars are waged in the minds of men and women in the world, they produce psychoses, neuroses, fears, and anxieties. Multiply individual strife by millions, and there is a world war.

What good does it do to abolish the external conditions of war, if the internal conditions of selfishness, hatred of neighbor, bigotry and intolerance and forgetfulness of God continue to exist? Wars are not caused solely by aggression or tyranny from without, for unless there had been the spirit of selfishness in some minds there could never be aggression. Nothing ever happens in the world that does not happen first inside human hearts. War is actually a projection of our own wickedness; our forgetfulness of God has more to do with war than is generally believed.

God has implanted certain laws in the universe by which things attain their proper perfection. These laws are principally of two kinds: natural laws and moral laws.

What we call the natural laws, such as the laws of astronomy and the laws of physics and the laws of biology, are in reality so many reflections of the Eternal Reason of God. God made things to act in a certain way. In this sense the oak is a judgment on the acorn; the harvest is a judgment on the seed that was sown.

But God did not make man like the sun, which can only rise and set. Having made man free, He gave him a higher law than the natural law, namely, the *moral law.* Fire *must* obey the natural law of its nature, but man merely *ought* to obey the moral law. His freedom gives him the license to rebel.

God's purpose in imposing law on *things* was to lead them *necessarily* to their perfection; and God's purpose in giving man the moral law was to lead him *freely* to his perfection.

To the extent that we obey God's will we are happy and at peace; to the extent that we freely disobey it, we hurt ourselves—and this consequence we call judgment.

Judgments are clear in the natural order. For example, a headache is a judgment on my refusal to eat, which is a law of nature; and atrophy of muscles is a judgment on my refusal to exercise.

Disobedience to these laws entails certain consequences, not because we will those consequences, but because of the very nature of the reality which God made.

No one who overdrinks wills the headache, but he gets one; no man who sins wills frustration or loneliness of soul, but he feels it. In breaking a law we always suffer certain consequences which we never intended. God so made the world that certain effects follow certain causes.

When calamity comes upon us, as a consequence of our neglect or defiance of God's will, that is what we call the judgment of God. The world does not will this war, but it wills a way of life which produces it; and in that sense, it is a judgment of God. Sin brings adversity, and adversity is the expression of God's condemnation of evil, the registering of Divine Judgment.

The frustration resulting from our disobedience to God's law is His judgment. And in disobeying God's moral law, we do not destroy it—we only destroy ourselves. For example, I am free to misuse the law of gravitation by jumping off a building, but in doing so, I kill myself—and the law still stands.

Let me tell you a little story, a story told to me by a missionary from Tonga Island. A chief of a nearby island came to visit the missionary and asked him to build him a motorboat. The missionary said, "I will build you a boat on one condition, that you give me nothing material. All I want is the right to go to your island and try to save a few souls."

Four months later, when the boat was finished, the missionary took it to the island. The chief and all of his people met the missionary and prepared a great feast. Four pigs were barbecued and stretched out on clean mats covered with luscious fruits. The chief gave a speech, thanking the missionary. The missionary said, "I am a little disappointed. I came here for souls, and I find none." With that the chief gestured. In that part of the world, people always gesture by moving the index finger downward and not upward as we do here. The chief motioned for his thirteen-year-old daughter Kasa, and then said to the missionary, "I relinquish my daughter; she is now yours. Take her with you." The missionary took her back to Tonga and put her in school, where she was educated until she was twenty-one years of age. She then asked to become a nun. The missionary refused: "No! You may not become a nun now. You go back to your own people and stay there one year; then at the end of that time, if you still feel that you have the vocation, you may come back and we will consider your desire to enter the convent."

So it was agreed; she went back to her own people. Shortly after her arrival, her father died. She baptized him on his deathbed. Her mother died later on, and she baptized the mother, and she then converted her brother, whose name was Low Gear. This is one effect of the GI's in the Pacific. The natives picked up words they heard them use and gave them to their children. The same missionary told me that he unearthed in his trunk, an old union suit, the long-handlebar type, and gave it to a native called Benzine. The following Sunday, Benzine came to church and walked down the middle aisle wearing the long underwear!

To return to our story, after Low Gear became a Christian, there suddenly broke out on the island persecution and bigotry. The natives ridiculed the virtue of Kasa, beat and tortured and ostracized her; this went on for months and months.

One day many of the natives were down at the shore, watching men diving into the sea to spear fish. Suddenly the water became crimson with blood, bits of human flesh floated to the surface. One of the sons of the woman who was most bitter against Kasa was devoured by a shark. Immediately the islanders began shouting, shrieking and raising their arms, crying, "Jahve! Why hast Thou done so to us? Jahve! What have we done? Jahve! Why should we suffer?" Jahve is the Hebrew name for God. How did these people ever know the Hebrew name for God? That we cannot answer. What is interesting is, they sought a reason for the catastrophe. They suspected they had done something to bring down the Judgment of God on them. Finally, one of them said, "Is it because of the way we treated Kasa?"

"Yes," the rest shouted, "that is it." The girl went back to Tonga Island and became Sister Gabriel. Returning later to her own native island, she is now educating them and bringing them the consolations of faith.

These people may be closer to the truth than we are, when they attribute crisis to an infraction of the moral law of God.

In disobeying His Will, we destroy ourselves. In stabbing Him, it is our own heart we slay. By catastrophes must we sadly learn that the moral law is right, and will prevail.

Fire burns, therefore let us not stick our hands in it; Godlessness causes war, therefore let us be Godly.

All nations and all peoples must learn, in sorrow and tears and blood and sweat, that wrong attitudes toward the natural law and the moral law are simultaneously and necessarily a wrong attitude toward God, and therefore bring inevitable doom, which is the Judgment of God.

CHAPTER THREE

# Science, Relativity, and the Atomic Bomb

On December 2, 1942, under the West Stadium of Stagg Field of the University of Chicago, the first atomic fire in the history of the world was lighted. Our atomic era began. Since that day some have blamed science for revealing such destructive powers in the atom. Against this and other false charges, we would say a word in defense of science.

In recent years, science has been attacked on the ground that it is atheistic and godless, and it is unconcerned with ethical and moral values.

Science is not atheistic and godless. Physical science is not concerned with God, or religion, or moral values. It is just as wrong to accuse empirical science of being atheistic as to accuse a speaker of being anti-American because in his speech he does not quote the Constitution of the United States. Maybe the Constitution did not fit under the subject he was discussing. Neither do God nor ethics fall under physics or chemistry.

Remember that every science is based upon an abstraction. An abstraction is taking a point of view or looking at things under a certain aspect or from a particular angle. All sciences are differentiated by their abstraction.

This diagram illustrates how sciences are based on different abstractions. A man is jumping off the bridge into the

river. Suppose a physicist, a psychologist, and a theologian all look at this man falling. Each of them looks at the jumper from a particular point of view, which makes up his science. The physicist says, "Now that is a very interesting phenomenon, watching that man fall. Here I see exemplified the law of falling bodies. He is going to fall 32 feet the first second and 64 feet the second second. Given the height of the bridge as 100 feet above the water, I must figure out how long it will take him to hit the water." The physicist must not be condemned for not considering the motivation which induced the man to jump. Such a problem is outside the scope of his science.

The psychologist looks at him and says to himself, "I wonder why he jumped? Maybe he had a fight with his wife; maybe the income-tax collector caught up with him; or perhaps his mother-in-law moved in." He could think of a thousand and one other motives which inspired the act. But the psychologist must not be condemned for ignoring any but a psychological problem.

The theologian looks at him, and says, "I wonder if he made an act of contrition before he hit the water?" His concern is whether he died in a state of sin or in union with God.

This reminds me of a story of a woman who went to the saintly John Vianney, the Curé of Ars. Her husband had jumped from a bridge. Using tragedy to impress the Curé, she said, "My husband died a double death: a death of body and a death of soul." The saint answered, "Remember, madam, there is a little distance between the bridge and the water." In other words, he had time to make an act of contrition. There is a chance for all of us.

Apply this to the physical scientist. He is interested in the universe only in terms of its quantity and its motion expressed principally in mathematics, or in what are called "pointer readings." God and religion are outside the scope of his science, and it is as unfair to accuse the scientist, *as a scientist*, of being atheistic as it is to accuse him of being anti-British. He might very well be anti-British, but not because he is a physical scientist. He conceivably might be atheistic, but he is not atheistic because he is a scientist. He might be atheistic because he is a fellow traveler of Communism. Poetry is outside of the domain of physics as such. So are God and morality. It is as unfair, therefore, to say science is atheistic as to say it is antipoetic. The science of a religious man must be scientific; the religion of a scientific man must be religious.

Great credit then to our scientists for their discoveries, and in particular for the acumen and learning behind the theory of relativity. In order to understand how the theory developed, picture a man swimming in a river with a strong current.

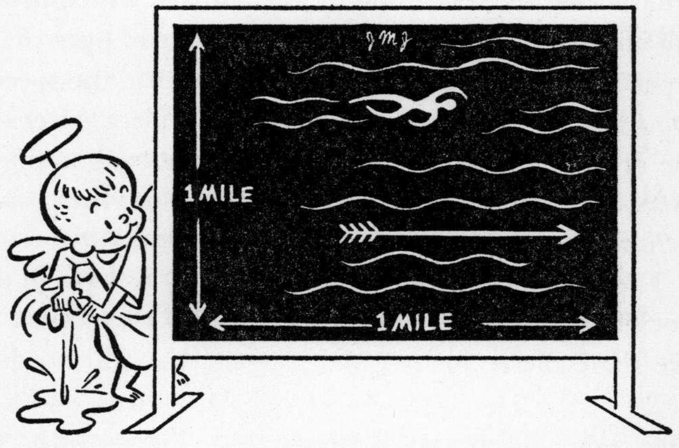


Suppose he swims first a mile down the river with the current, and then a mile up against the current. After he finishes it down and back, he swims across the river, over and back, the distance being one mile each way. It will take a shorter time to swim the two miles back and forth across the current than the two miles up and down, with the current and against it, because, though the man's speed increases with the current, nevertheless swimming upstream meets with such resistance that it requires a longer time. Such in any case is the theory of it, given a very strong current.

Is it not very reasonable for scientists to say, "Let us do this with the universe. Let us send out a ray of light in the direction of the earth's ether and back again, and then at right angles to it"? To do this, Michelson and Morley of Western Reserve University constructed in 1887 a machine called an "interferometer." It was simply four crossbars, with mirrors at the end of each bar. Since light travels at a rate of over 186,000 miles per second, the way they had to measure the speed of the going and the return was on photographic plate. After sending the ray of light out with the current and back again, and then across the current and back, they found out there was no difference. They knew there should have been, but there was none. The swimmer in the water and the ray of light in ether did not produce the same results. They said there must be a mistake somewhere. So they did it again, but still no difference.

Two other scientists, Kennedy and Illingsworth, tried many times. Still there was no difference. Two other scientists offered explanations—first Lorenz and then Fitzgerald, an Irishman, who got most of the credit for it.

Now physicists speak of the "Fitzgerald law of contraction." He tried to explain why no difference was registered; he said that the length of objects contracts with speed. For example, if you increase the speed of a ship in water, you can imagine that the boat is pulling itself together just the least little bit. If a heavyweight fighter hit you, you would "pull" up the least little bit, and not measure as much as you did before. Fitzgerald held that a measuring rod shortens as the speed increases. The reason is because the electrical particles inside it are set in motion by new magnetic forces. The contraction depends, not on the stuff of which the rod is made, but on the velocity. There should have been a difference in the speed with the ether and at right angles to it, but, because of the contraction of the measuring rod and the great speed in the direction of the current, the difference was neutralized.

Scientists confirmed the Fitzgerald law of contraction. If you take a measuring rod, for example, from the earth to the sun, whose speed is 19 miles per second, the measuring rod will contract 1/200,000,000 part, or a distance of 2½ inches in relationship to the diameter of the earth. Experiments further revealed that the mass of an electron contracts with speed.

Then came Einstein, who said, "Measurement varies with speed. But if measurement varies with speed, then space is relative to speed; then time is relative to speed; then measurements are relative to speed; in other words, space and time are relative."

A foot rule on the earth is longer than a foot rule on the sun. Space and time will be relative to the speed of the planet on which we place our measuring rod.

The general theory of relativity, in its most simple terms, is that space and time are relative to the observer. But what is always kept constant is the speed of light. Einstein said that the theory could be wrong, but please God it is not, otherwise the scientists are going to have a terrible time of it. Poor Fitzgerald, too, would be knocked completely out of the picture!

Do we find it difficult to imagine that space and time are relative? You listen to me for about six minutes trying to describe the theory. It seems like an hour to you. If you were listening to Milton Berle for one hour, it would seem like a minute. That is relativity of time.

Now, for an example of relativity of space. From an airplane your uncle looks like an "ant."

A second charge that has been hurled against science is that science is a Frankenstein monster, which creates an atomic bomb to destroy mankind. Science is not to be blamed for the atomic bomb; science is interested only in the discovery of the secrets of nature. What is discovered may be abused, but that does not mean the discovery was evil. When man discovered fire, there was a danger. He put fire into the hearth to warm the home, but it could also burn down his home. When man discovered the fermentation of wine, there was a danger of alcoholism. But the fermentation of wine is good even though some men drink too much of it. But the abuse does not take away the right to use it lawfully. Many cut themselves with knives, but we should not throw all knives into a pit. The discovery of atomic energy is good—that is the way that God lights the world; light and heat are produced in the sun through atomic fission. Since God put atomic energy in the sun, more power to the minds who discovered the great truth. The scientists who revealed its secrets did not do so in order to destroy. It is indeed regrettable that the first general knowledge the world had of atomic energy was when it wiped out a Japanese city. Morse's first message by telegraph was to praise God, not to deny Him. The first use of electrical energy was not to electrocute a man.

When we speak of the atomic bomb, we must make a distinction between atomic energy and an atomic bomb. The energy is a gift of God. As far back as August, 1941, an article appeared in a scientific journal on atomic fission. The government requested the journalists and the newspapers not to publish anything about atomic fission in the United States; the journalists kept that pledge. But in February, 1943, two years before the first atomic bomb exploded, there was an address given before the Pontifical Academy of Science by Pope Pius XII, in which he said, "Means have now been discovered to smash atoms through neutrons released by radioactivity. . . .

"It has now been calculated that one cubic meter of oxide powder of uranium can, in 1/100 of a second, lift the weight of one billion pounds, sixteen miles in the air."

Then he pleaded: "I hope that this atomic energy will always be used for constructive purposes, and that means will be found to use it for the advance of civilization. If, however, it is ever used destructively, it will bring great harm to the places where it is used, and there may result a terrible catastrophe for the planet itself."

He was speaking not as a scientist, but merely pronouncing a moral judgment about the use of atomic energy. But it coincides with the statement of Lindbergh: "We know that within the next decade it will be technically possible to assemble weapons which can destroy every city in the world within a few hours after the start of the war. There are alarming indications that the possessors of modern scientific knowledge may be able to destroy all life over large areas of the earth's surface. Some scientists have predicted that man will gain the power to detonate the planet itself."

The discovery of this energy brings to us the problem of how it shall be used. Shall it be used as energy to turn the wheels of industry or to occasion cosmic suicide?

The use of atomic energy brings us back again to the Greek legend of Prometheus and the age-old problem of whether force should be used against law.

Prometheus steals fire from Heaven, but when he finds that this fire is used as a force against law, he turns against those to whom he brought it, and defends the rights of Zeus, who is the God Almighty.

> All crooked plans they turned to mirth in their great hearts,
> And thought full easily by strength to master all.

The question before man today is whether he will use this power for destruction or use it for purposes of peace. It often happens in the history of the world that great benefits flow from restraint, such as the denying of oneself the eating of a fruit which stands for a knowledge of evil as well as good. There is sometimes a tree from which it is man's business *not to eat;* there are things which he ought to forswear to use, lest they increase the evil of the world.

If the troubles of our world are *outside* of us—socially and economically—we shall have to submit to a cruel fate indeed. If the trouble with the world lies *inside* the human heart, then it is possible to remedy all that trouble. We can remedy it by returning again to the great tradition of our Founding Fathers, of being once more a religious people, loving our neighbor, our country, and serving God.

CHAPTER FOUR

# The Yearnings of the Pre-Christian World

Every now and then someone boasts, "I have an absolutely new idea." Three answers may be given. One is "Treat it kindly, it is in a strange place." The other is "Beginner's luck." And the third and best answer is "Go back and see how the ancients put it." Very often we call something modern because we do not know what is ancient; many so-called "modern" ideas are really old errors with new labels. We owe a greater debt to the past than is generally recognized. The waters of ancient cultures are constantly washing our shores.

It may be interesting to make a survey of a thousand years of pre-Christian history and delve into the yearnings, the aspirations, the hope and anticipation of some of the great peoples of the past, beginning with the Greeks, then the Eastern world, and finally the Hebrews.

One of the greatest epic poets who ever lived was Homer, whom Plato called the educator of the Greeks. Homer wrote two great works, one called the *Iliad* and the other the *Odyssey*. The *Iliad* ends with the story of a defeated king and the *Odyssey* with the story of a sorrowful woman. The first poem ends with a beautiful tribute paid to Hector as one of the greatest of Trojan heroes. In the other poem, the *Odyssey*, which is concerned with Odysseus traveling about the world, there is the story of his wife, who was courted by many suitors. She said that when she finished weaving a particular garment, she would then decide on a suitor. The suitors did not know that each night Penelope undid the stitches that she put in during the daytime and thus remained faithful to Odysseus until he returned. Great classical scholars like Christopher Hollis have wondered why Homer threw into the current of literature the story of a king who was made great in defeat and a woman glorious in sadness and tragedy. Greek philosophy was concerned with answering this question. As Chesterton put it, "The role of Hector anticipates all the defeats through which our race and religion were to pass." It was impossible for all the Greek philosophers to understand how there could be victory in defeat, how there could be nobility in suffering. There was really no answer given to this problem until the day of Calvary, when a defeated man hanging on a Cross ultimately became the conqueror, and a Mater Dolorosa at the foot of the Cross became the Queen of Christendom.

Over 500 years before the Christian era lived the great dramatist Aeschylus, who wrote *Prometheus Bound*. Prometheus is pictured as bound to a rock because he had stolen fire from Heaven. An eagle comes and devours his entrails—a symbol of modern man, whose heart is being devoured, not by an eagle, but by anxiety and fear, neuroses and psychoses. For these thousands of years mankind had been yearning for some kind of deliverance; that aspiration found its answer in the speech of Hermes to Prometheus, "Look not for any end, moreover, to this curse, until some God appears to accept upon his head, the pangs of thy own sins vicarious."

In the second dialogue of Alcibiades one reads that as Alcibiades was about to go into the temple, he came to Socrates, the wise man, and said, "What shall I ask of the gods?" And Socrates said, "Wait! Wait for a wise man who is to come, who will tell us how we are to conduct ourselves before God and man." Alcibiades said, "I am ready to do all He desires. When will He come?"

Socrates said, "I know not when, but I know that He also desires your good."

But Greek literature was not alone in picturing man craving for another wisdom than that of earth, and another relief from inner misery than that given by man alone.

The Eastern people had it, too. The ancient Hindus sacrificed a lamb to Ekiam as they prayed, "When will the Saviour come? When will the Redeemer appear?" Their avatars were not incarnations, but rather a descent of *deities* to the realm of man, such as Krishna, a deity who visited humanity, Bhagavad-Gita, who became a brother to all men, and Brahma, who was often pictured as one who would repair the faults of Kaliga, the ancient serpent.

Confucius in his *Morals* continued this universal craving for a Saviour when he wrote, "The Holy One must come from heaven who will know all things and have power over heaven and earth."

One may ask if Buddha pointed to Christ? Buddha, the founder of Buddhism, lived from 563 to 483 B.C. On dying he said, "I am not the first Buddha who came upon earth, nor shall I be the last. I will die, but Buddha will live, for Buddha is Truth. The Kingdom of truth will increase for about 500 years. . . . In due time another Buddha will arise and he will reveal to you the self-same eternal truth which I have taught." His disciple Ananda asked, "How shall we know him?" Buddha answered, "The Buddha who will come after me will be known as Maitreya, which means, 'He whose name is Love.' "

Roman civilization struck the same chord, for all humanity is one. After answering that philosophy based on self-sufficiency was not sufficient, they craved for some inner purification; this prompted them to develop mystery religions. These cults led to many excesses, but their *subjective dispositions* were right, inasmuch as they saw man must have mystery as well as philosophy.

Cicero, the great orator, quotes a sibyl as saying, "A King will come who must be recognized to be saved." Then Cicero asks, "Of what man and of what time did the sibyl speak?" In Latin, his question was:

*In quem hominem?*

Was that question answered by another Roman?

*Ecce Homo!*—"Behold the Man."

Suetonius, in his life of Augustus, continued the traditional aspiration: "Nature has been in labor to bring forth a personage who would be King of the Romans." The Senate was disturbed by this general expectation and passed a law forbidding anyone to let live a male child *that year*. The order was not executed because many of the senators' wives were with child. But it did show how much the ancient air was filled with a hushed expectancy that some great King was coming to the world.

Tacitus confirmed this in his *History:* "Mankind is generally persuaded that the ancient prophecies of the East will prevail, and it will not be long until Judea would bring forth one who would rule the universe."

Horace in his "Sixteenth Epode" has the Golden World on the far western seas, bidding his readers emigrate there to escape the hopeless horror of reality. Virgil's eclogue answers, "No, the golden age is here," for in the year 31 B.C. he wrote the "Fourth Eclogue" to honor Augustus. This poem has through the centuries been looked upon as Messianic, and recent studies at Oxford favor that judgment. . . . *Iam nova progenies caelo demittitur alto:* "Already a new generation is being sent down from high heaven."

Virgil lived in a world which gave no great dignity to woman. Yet in this poem, after describing the "promise of a Jove about to be" and the child as yet unborn, the last four lines speak to the child as already born. *Incipe, parve puer, Risu cognoscere matrem:* "Begin, little child, to recognize your mother with a smile."

And now as these expectations multiply, the greatest of them all is the Hebrew. The Hebrew civilization was destroyed by the King of Babylon in the year 586 B.C. He had taken back with him into Babylon one who was called the wisest and the most handsome of the Jews, Daniel. The King had a dream one night that neither he nor any of his aides could interpret. In the dream he saw a great and tremendous colossus. The head was of gold; the breast and arms were of silver, the belly and thighs were of brass, and the feet were part iron and part clay. And the great stones hewn from the mountains without hands, came from the mountains, struck it in the feet of clay, and ground it into dust.

Since his own sages could not tell the meaning, Daniel was summoned by the King to interpret it: "These are the kingdoms that will divide the world until the coming of the expected One of the world." "The empire of gold," he said, "is you. You will fall and be devoured by the empire of silver; the empire of silver will, in its turn, be conquered by the empire of brass; and the empire of brass will go down before the empire of iron and clay."

In the year 538 B.C., the Medes and Persians came to this great city of Babylon, which was sixteen miles square, with sixteen gates of solid bronze giving entrance to it. Cyrus turned aside the waters of the Euphrates, which ran through the center of the city, and went into it under the walls in the dry bed of the river. That night Baltazaar was slain, and the empire of gold was taken over by the empire of silver.

Then there arises a new power—the empire of brass. Trained in their games, knowing where to hazard and when to abandon, the Greeks now arose to swallow up the Persians, as the Persians had swallowed the Chaldeans. Greece could not bear the thought of being subdued by Asia. Every Greek prepared to defend his liberty, and the only dispute among them was who should do more for the public. Then arose the great Alexander of the Greeks; brave as Darius III was, he could not stop either the genius or the arms of the great Greek, who carried his conquests into every land of the Persians and at thirty-three years of age was destined to show the vanity of all earthly glory. Sighing for new worlds to conquer, he little suspected that, at that age, the one world left to conquer and the only one worth conquering was the next. He died without leisure to settle his affairs and left his ambition to a simpleton brother. It was the first great war between Europe and Asia.

The beasts of paganism were devouring one another. The last great empire which God prepared now was ready to appear on the stage of the world's history. It was the mightiest of all! Rome, the empire of iron, looked to Greece and Carthage as its prey. Rome's screaming eagles went to war. Dragging her ponderous battering rams like chains, shaking the earth like marching mountains, her unbridled horses darting like hawks, the Romans moved on, while there came from ten thousand times ten thousand throats the cry of hate: *Delenda est Carthago!* "Carthage must be destroyed." Rome under Scipio went to battle, and Carthage fell finally in 146 B.C. as nothing has fallen since Satan fell from heaven.

Rome became supreme. With her arms of iron, she crushed the agonizing kingdoms of the world, one after another. The world was at peace. There was nothing more to conquer. The Temple of Janus, which was kept open to pray for success in war, and which was closed only twice in seven hundred years, was now closed again. Perhaps its doors were clogged with the dead bodies of its citizens. In any case the world was at peace, and it was prophesied the King of Men would be born when the world no longer bore arms or went to battle.

Caesar Augustus, now that the world was at peace, resolved to take a census of the greatest empire the world had ever known. In the great hall of his palace by the Tiber, he, the master bookkeeper of the world, was casting up the accounts of the nations of the earth. Before him stretched on a frame was a chart labeled laconically: *Orbis terrarum—Imperium Romanum:* "The circle of the earth—the Roman Empire." A careful and thrifty man was Augustus, the Caesar of the earth. No one should escape the census, for Rome was the mistress of all. From the western ocean to the Persian plains, from the frozen north to the edge of the southern desert the list went out from his hand to every sweating governor and satrap and tetrarch and king. The world is to be brought to unity. The human race had only one capital: Rome; one master: Caesar; one language: Latin. Morally the world was one in its sin and corruption; materially it was one, for it had reached the highest peak of organization and unity. There are no longer Medes or Persians, no longer Scythians or barbarians, no longer Greeks or Babylonians. There are only Romans; there are only men. Nations were not awaiting a king, but rather mankind was awaiting a king.

Little did the bookkeeper of the Tiber know that he was aiding in the fulfillment of the Jewish prophet Micheas that the "Expected of the Nations" would be born in Bethlehem. The census notice was finally posted in the little village of Nazareth that a carpenter might read it—he who belonged to the defunct royalty of the family of David, whose city was Bethlehem. He and his espoused wife Mary journeyed to Bethlehem.

"But there was no room at the inn"; the inn is the gathering place of public opinion; so often public opinion locks its doors to the King. Out to the stables they go. There rings out over the softness of the evening breeze a cry, a gentle cry, the cry of a newborn baby. The sea could not hear the cry, for the sea was filled with its own voice. The great ones of the earth could not hear the cry, for they could not understand how God could be greater than a man.

Wise men came from the East, perhaps Persia. They saw the Babe—a Babe Whose tiny hands were not quite long enough to touch the huge heads of the cattle, and yet hands that were steering the reins that keep the sun, moon, and stars in their orbits. Shepherds came, and they saw baby lips that did not speak, and yet lips that might have articulated the secret of every living man that hour. They saw a baby brow under which was a mind and intelligence compared with which the combined intelligences of Europe and America amount to naught.

The Babe could not walk, because those baby feet could not bear the weight of Divine Omnipotence. Eternity is in time; Omnipotence in bonds; God in the form of man. The yearnings of Buddha, of Confucius, of Aeschylus, of Virgil, of Socrates, of Plato—all were now realized in a Child in the stable. *Incipe, parve puer:* "Begin, little Child, to recognize Thy mother with a smile."

## CHAPTER FIVE

# The Infinity of Littleness

No old people ever enter the Kingdom of Heaven. The Divine Lord put it this way: "Unless you become as a little child, you cannot enter the Kingdom of Heaven." In an age of sophistication and pride, it might be well to learn the advantages of littleness or humility.

See how important it is in the physical order: In order to see anything big, one must be physically little. A child's world is always immense. To every boy, his father is the biggest man in all the world, and his uncle, who is standing alongside of a window, is taller than the oak tree in the yard beyond. Every child loves the story of "Jack and the Beanstalk." The beanstalk to a child actually towers to the sky; giants are the creation of humility. A little boy can put himself on a broomstick, and it is not long until he imagines himself "clinging to the whistling mane of every wind," riding the rough savannahs of the blue.

Every little girl finds her doll a child who draws out from her, her deep maternal instincts. A boy will receive a gift of tin soldiers. They are really only three inches high; but once he puts them on the carpet and lines them up in battle array, he hears the rat-tat-tat of machine guns and smells the smoke of battle; the red of the carpet becomes the blood of the battle fire as poppy fields are turned into Haceldamas of blood. It is a real war, until he becomes a man; then he sweeps away into the attic all of his little tin soldiers with all of the childhood fancies, and the world becomes very small. As he ceases to be little, his world shrinks in size. Giants begin to dwarf, broomsticks and wooden guns lose their romance, dolls cease to be children needing a mother's attention. Life's greatest joys depart when they are carted away.

What does it mean to be a child? Francis Thompson said that it meant living in a nutshell, counting yourself the king of infinite space. "It means to be able to turn pumpkins into coaches, and mice into horses, and to get gold dusty from tumbling among the stars. It means, also, to sit in the lap of Mother Nature and twine her tresses a thousand wilful ways to see in which fashion she will look the most beautiful." That is what it means to be a child.

Carry the law to a higher level. If physical littleness is the condition of seeing the world big, then spiritual littleness or humility is the condition of discovering Infinite Truth and Love. No man discovers anything big unless he makes himself small. If he magnifies his ego to infinity, he will learn nothing, for there is nothing bigger than the infinite. If he reduces his ego to zero and is no longer proud and conceited, then he will discover everything big, even bigger than himself. His world begins to be infinite. In order to discover truth, goodness and justice, and God, one must be very humble.

If a box is filled with salt, it cannot be filled with pepper. If we are filled with our own importance, then we can never be filled with anything outside of ourselves. If a man thinks he knows everything, then not even God can teach him anything.

The discovery of any truth requires docility, or teachableness. He who thinks he knows it all is unteachable. Notice how very calm and passive a scientist is before nature. He just sits and looks at nature. He waits for nature to tell him its laws. He does not say, "I know the laws of nature, and I am going to impose my laws upon nature." Rather, he waits upon the revelation of nature. The humility of the scientist before nature ought to be the attitude of man before God, awaiting His Holy Will. Faith comes from hearing, which also means it

comes from being a good listener, or not thinking that one has all truth within himself.

The illustration you were just looking at was the sun and its rays. There was a man walking away from the sun. Notice that the shadow fell ahead of him. I gave him a big head, because he is swelled-headed about himself and believes that he is just as big as his shadow, which is only a phantom self, not the real self. Let the sun stand for God and the Light of His Truth. As long as we walk away from God, we create psychological shadows. We believe ourselves different from what we are. But notice the difference when we walk toward the sun or Divine Light; then the fantasy can never be mistaken for the real self because it falls behind us. Once we put ourselves directly under the sun, we are completely governed by Divine Truth; there are no shadows at all, no illusions, no shadowy fears, no nocturnal anxieties; rather a peace and calm pervades the soul. Being humble implies that our eye recognizes the need of light, our reason admits the need of faith, and our whole being the guidance of the Eternal Law of God.

What is in humility which corresponds to childlikeness? Humility is not servility, not a readiness to be walked on, not a hatred of self, not psychological self-contempt, not a desire to be placed at a disadvantage. Humility is the virtue that tells us the *truth about ourselves*, that is, how we stand, not in the eyes of men, but before God. It is not underestimation: a tall person is not being humble if, when complimented on his height, he says, "Oh! No! Really, I am only six feet three." A great singer is not humble when she says, "Oh! No! My 'collateral notes' are abominable." But she is humble if she says, "Thanks, but I owe it all to God."

The truth about ourselves can be denied in two ways: by overestimation and by underestimation. We overestimate our worth when we say, "I am a better American than anyone in this city." On the other hand, people sometimes call themselves stupid that others may say they are wise. I once heard a retort made to a person who was always calling himself stupid; his friend said, "Did you really have to mention that fact?"

Humility in relation to love means thinking others better than ourselves. One advantage of this is that it gives us some examples to imitate. Pride, on the other hand, sometimes seeks first place that others may say, "Oh! What greatness!" Pride, too, can subtly take the *last* place that others may say, "What humility!"

(Notice how quickly our angel cleans the blackboard. The reason is that every angel lives in dread of being knocked back to a cherub.)

Why is it that beggars always use tin cups? It is because they appeal to the vanity of the giver who likes to hear the clink of the coin in the cup. In churches we always use plush-bottomed collection baskets because people should seek to make no noise when they give, but let it be known to God alone.

Pride even gets into so-called "pious" people who boast of their piety. I once heard a very interesting story about Father Vaughn. Father Vaughn was a great preacher of a generation or so ago in England. He was on top of a London bus one day, reading his Breviary. A Breviary is a book of devotions we have to say every day, and it is made up for the most part of selections from the Old and New Testaments, the lives of the saints, hymns and prayers. It takes about an hour each day to fulfill the obligation.

Father Vaughn was reading his Breviary on top of the London bus, and someone seated near him shouted for the hearing of everyone, "Look at this! Here is the great Father Vaughn who gets on top of a London bus, takes out a prayer book, and begins praying so that everyone will notice and think he is good."

The man continued, "When I pray, I follow the injunction of the Scriptures. I close the door, go into my closet, and pray alone to the Father."

Father Vaughn then answered, "And then you get on top of a London bus and tell the world about it."

The golfer, too, is full of pride who smashes his club and says, "That was a rotten shot." By that he means "This is really not my normal game." One golfer said, "I have not been on my normal game for thirty years."

Suppose someone came to me after this telecast, saying, "That was a nice television show." If I retorted, "Really it was nothing; I spent only three minutes preparing it," that would be pride. I would be implying, "Just think of what the show would be if I spent *four* minutes preparing it."

The critical spirit is another fruit of pride. People who are very proud often have many things wrong with them on the inside, such as selfishness and conceit. As a result their conscience bothers them, because of their submerged guilt, which they refuse to face. Instead of criticizing themselves, which they ought to do, they project the criticism to others. They reform others instead of themselves, point out the mote in the eye of others without seeing the beam in their own. Why is it that so many newspapers specialize in murder stories, adulteries, infidelities, and disloyalty? Because when others read about a murder or a robbery, they say, "I am not that bad; really I am pretty good." They establish comparisons and console themselves on being much better than their neighbors. Abraham Lincoln was once entering a hospital when a young man, not looking where he was running, bumped into Lincoln and knocked him prone on the floor. The young man to defend himself shouted, "You long-legged fool, why don't you get out of people's way?" Lincoln, knowing human nature well, looked up at him, asking, "Young man, what's troubling you on the *inside?*"

Walter Winchell once consoled a victim of criticism and slander by saying, "Remember that nobody will ever get ahead of you as long as he is kicking you in the seat of the pants." It is a physical impossibility.

Pride generally denies personal responsibility for wrongdoing. Most people deny they are sinners. The tragedy of this is they never feel the need of a Saviour. The blind man who denies he is blind never wants to see. I heard of two social workers who denied personal guilt. They were discussing a criminal, and one of them admitted, "I know he committed murder and robbed a bank and all that, but remember, he was an orphan."

The other social worker said, "Yes, but he was an orphan because he shot his parents at the age of nine."

The first social worker answered, "I know it, but he did it in self-defense."

The modern god can be the ego, or self. This is atheism. Pride is inordinate self-love, an exaltation of the conditional and relative self into an absolute. It tries to gratify the thirst for the infinite by giving to one's own finitude a pretension to divinity. In some, pride blinds the self to its weakness and becomes "hot" pride; in others, it recognizes its own weakness and overcomes it by a self-exaltation which becomes "cold" pride. Pride kills docility and makes a man incapable of ever being helped by God. The limited knowledge of the puny mind pretends to be final and absolute. In the face of other intellects, it resorts to two techniques, either the technique of omniscience, by which it seeks to convince others how much it knows, or the technique of *nescience*, which tries to convince others how little they know. When such pride is unconscious, it becomes almost incurable, for it identifies truth with *its* truth. Pride is an admission of weakness; it secretly fears all competition and dreads all rivals. It is rarely cured when the person himself is vertical—*i.e.*, healthy and prosperous; but it can be cured when the patient is horizontal—sick and disillusioned. That is why catastrophes are necessary in an era of pride to bring men back again to God and the salvation of their souls.

Did you ever think of the greatest act of humility this world ever knew? An analogy may help us understand it. Suppose you were saddened by the way dogs were treated, beaten by strangers, starved, and driven from the company of men.

To teach mankind to love dogs, further suppose that you divested your body and put your soul into the body of a dog. That would mean that inside the organism of a dog was an intellect capable of knowing God and a will capable of loving Him. Suppose that when you took on the form and habit of a dog, you resolved never to transcend the limitations of that animal organism. Though you had a mind that could scan the infinite, you would never speak, you would not utter a word but would limit yourself to a bark. Though you were an artist, you would not use a brush to create. Second, suppose you resolved to subject yourself only to the companionship of other dogs, sharing their lives just in an effort to try and help them in virtue of your superior mind. That would indeed be an act of humility and a humiliation, particularly if you died defending the animals whose nature you embraced in order to save.

That gives us a faint idea of something that really happened. Think of God becoming man. Suppose He first took on himself a human nature like unto ours in all things save sin. In doing so, He subjected Himself to two limitations. Though He was the Word, He would speak in words; though He had a Mind which embraced eternity, He chose to speak in the dull tongue that human intellects could understand. Not only that, suppose further that because He took on human form,

He would not forgo companionship with men but would become a victim to their abuse, their misunderstanding, their scorn, and their cruelties. That indeed would be humiliation. If you think that it would be humiliating for a human spirit to go into the organism of an animal, what do you think it would be like for an Infinite God to descend into the form of a man? That actually happened, and such is the meaning of the Babe in the manger of Bethlehem.

By meditating on how God humbled Himself to become a man and then died to save us, we become little children in the spiritual sense, and the world becomes so big, so romantic, so full of mystery. From such humble hearts comes wonderment such as Thompson expressed to the God Who became a Babe:

Little Jesus, wast Thou shy
Once, and just so small as I?
And what did it feel like to be
Out of Heaven, and just like me?
Didst Thou sometimes think of there,
And ask where all the angels were?
I should think that I would cry
For my house all made of sky;
I would look about the air,
And wonder where my angels were;
And at waking 'twould distress me—
Not an angel there to dress me.
Hadst Thou ever any toys,
Like us little girls and boys?
And didst Thou play in Heaven with all
The angels that were not too tall,
With stars for marbles? Did the things
Play "can you see me?" through their wings?

And did Thy Mother let Thee spoil
Thy robes, with playing on our soil?
How nice to have them always new
In Heaven, because 'twas quite clean blue.

Didst Thou kneel at night and pray,
And didst Thou join Thy hands, this way?
And did they tire sometimes, being young,
And make the prayer seem very long?
And dost Thou like it best that we
Should join our hands to pray to Thee?
And did Thy Mother at the night
Kiss Thee, and fold the clothes in right?
I used to think, before I knew,
The prayer not said unless we do.
And didst Thou feel quite good in bed,
Kissed and sweet, and Thy prayers said?
Thou canst not have forgotten all
That it feels like to be small;
And Thou know'st I cannot pray
To Thee in my father's way—
When Thou wast little, say,
Couldst Thou talk Thy Father's way?
So, a little child, come down
And hear a child's tongue like Thy own;
Take me by the hand and walk,
And listen to my baby talk.
To Thy Father show my prayer
(He will look, Thou art so fair)
And say: "O Father, I, Thy Son,
Bring the prayer of a little one."

And He will smile, that children's tongue
Has not changed since Thou wast young.

CHAPTER SIX

# How Mothers Are Made

There is a popular song which tells how boys and girls are made. "Girls," it is said, "are made of sugar and spice and everything nice. Boys are made of snips and snails and puppy dogs' tails."

But what are mothers made of? To answer that question we shall go a long way back, because it takes a long time to make a mother. In the cosmic preparation for motherhood three steps were necessary:

1. *Interiority of generation.* In the physical order, a flame lights a flame, a torch lights a torch. In lower forms of life, such as the amoeba, there is a fission, or splitting, as the young life breaks off from the parent cell. Motherhood is still a long way off, for there could never be a mother without an intimate, close, and vital relationship between the body of the mother and the body of the young offspring.

It took centuries to prepare for this interior act of generation. Some land crabs come down from the mountains to the sea, push their eggs into the water, and then abandon them. No real motherhood here, for the young never see their mothers, nor do the mothers care for the young. This universe of ours is full of orphans; the young that are begotten are completely forgotten. Almost all fruit is orphaned, inasmuch as it lives an independent existence from the tree. Butterflies are thoughtful to some extent, inasmuch as eggs are often hatched under a leaf, where they are least exposed. Maybe nature is kind to certain butterflies, for how shocked mothers would be to see a fuzzy-wuzzy, ugly caterpillar—the kind that only a mother could love. Hens are much kinder to the young—so kind that the Lord used them as an example of His concern for men:

> How often have I been ready to gather thy children together,
> As a hen gathers her chickens under her wings;
> And thou didst refuse it!

No boy who ever gathered eggs from the barnyard or a crib, as I did when I was a boy, will ever forget the wrath of a cackling, setting hen. You begin to know what an "old hen" is, when you go about gathering eggs. After all, you can't blame the hen; she can never find anything where she "lays" it.

As we see nature unfold, there is an increasing unity of mother and offspring until finally many mothers carry the young within them. Despite all this cosmic evolution, however, there could never be a human mother until love came into the world. Then alone would there be true interiority of generation. This would happen not as a result of seasonal urges and sex impulses alone, as it does in the animal order. In addition to sex, which is common to the animals, there must also be love, in order that there be no ravishing or stealing away of the worth of the person. If a mother is to be made, then what is begotten must come from a free act of the will, in which a woman freely submits to the love of a man. Such surrender would not be a passive one, like the earth to the seed, but rather an active one, in which two humans who are freely united in soul freely unite in body. One might almost say that the generation begins in the mind and in the soul with love and completes itself in the body.

All love tends to an incarnation, even God's. Generation, then, is not a push from below but a gift from above; it is a reflection of the Eternal Generation in the Bosom of the Father, Who in the agelessness of Eternity says, "Thou art My Son. This day have I begotten Thee." The roots of it are hidden in Heaven, for in the great Hebraic tradition we read a line wherein God speaks and says, "Shall I Who give generations to others, Myself be barren?" The offspring now is seen as the incarnation of the mutual love of a husband and a wife.

When a mother carries the young life within her through a free act of love, she has a different kind of love from what any man has for a neighbor. Most of us love a non-self, or something extrinsic and apart from our inner life; but a mother's love during the time she is a flesh-and-blood ciborium is not for a non-self but for one that is her very self, a perfect example of charity and love which hardly perceives a separation. Motherhood then becomes a kind of priesthood. She brings God to man by preparing the flesh in which the soul will be implanted; she brings man to God in offering the child back again to the Creator.

2. *Care of the young.* Mothers in the animal kingdom care only for a body; mothers in the spiritual kingdom must care also for a soul, a mind, and a heart. The soul comes from God and must go back again to Him. God sets the target, the parents are the bow, and their vocation is to shoot the arrow straight. When a child is given to his parents, a crown is made for that child in Heaven, and woe to the parents who raise a child without consciousness of that eternal crown!

It does not take long in the animal order to generate and develop the brain of a monkey, because the monkey brain does not have very much to do. But it takes a long time to develop the mind of a child, to inculcate ideals, virtues of purity, honesty, patriotism, and piety. Animals can quickly leave their parents, because they have no eternal destiny. But humanity is under a compulsory educational act, and to fulfill this, there must be domesticity. The home is the schoolhouse for affection wherein a mother completes the work that was begun when the child was born. Motherhood then turns into mother craft, as biology hands the work over to ethics. The canoe can quickly launch out on the waters when it is made, but the big ship has to wait for engines because it has a better port. A tiny ball of unconsciousness needs much mother care to become all that God destined it to be. Maybe that is why mothers are against war; they realize better than anyone else how long it takes to make a man.

3. *Greater attention to individuals of the species.* Mother love requires greater attention to individuals of the species. A mother must love each offspring as if it were the only one in all the world. This means recognizing that human beings are not just individuals, but persons. In the animal order there are *individuals;* in the human order there are *persons.* The difference between an individual and a person is this: individuals are replaceable, and persons are not. For example, you go to buy oranges in a store and say, "No, this one is bad. Give me another." But you cannot say that about children. A child is a person—unique, incommunicable, irreplaceable—that is why there is so much sorrow in a mother when one is lost. It is a person and an immortal soul that has departed.

This, incidentally, is why every mother gives to the child a name which implies dignity, uniqueness, and apartness. There is no greater refutation of Communism in the world than a mother. Because Communism denies the value of persons, it affirms that we are like grapes who have no other destiny than to have our life ground out of us for the sake of the collective wine of the state. Every mother arises to protest and proclaim, "This child of mine is a person and may not be submerged in any totality of a class or a state or a race; he is unique; he has a name; he is my son!"

That is how mothers are made. Nature had to prepare for them through millions of years by begetting a love that would freely desire children, a love that would educate them, and a love that would sacrifice for them because of their sovereign worth as persons endowed with immortal souls. Such love could not come from the beast, for that kind of love is a gift of God.

Motherhood is too noble to be without an ideal. God, Who became Man, preexisted His Own Mother, as an artist preexists his own painting. On one occasion, Whistler was complimented for the beautiful painting of his mother. His answer was, "You know how it is. One tries to make one's Mommy as nice as one can." There is no reason to feel that Christ would do otherwise, for, as God, He preexisted His Own Mother. That every mother might understand that the interior generation is born of love, She, the Ideal Mother, conceived because she cooperated with the Love of God. One day, out from the Great White Throne of Light, there came an Angel of Light who descended over the plains of Israel; passing by the daughters of great kings of the East, the Angel came to a woman who was kneeling in prayer and said, "Hail, full of grace." These were not words; they were the Word, and "The Word was made Flesh, and dwelt amongst us." And she, the Mother, was overshadowed by the Spirit of Love and bore within herself the Guest Who was really the Host of the World. This was the greatest love that the world ever knew—the Love that came down into a Woman and ended in an Incarnation.

This Mother gave further example to all mothers by caring both for the Body and the Soul of Her Son. She cared for His Body, for she wrapped Him in swaddling clothes and laid Him in a manger. She cared for His Soul and His Mind, for He was subject to her. What a lesson for children to learn! This Child, Who was subject to His Mother, was also the Creator of the world. Every mother, when she picks up the young life that has been born to her, looks up to the heavens to thank God for the gift which made the world young again. But here was a Mother, a Madonna, who did not look up. She looked down to Heaven, for This was Heaven in her arms.

Finally, she gave the example of the worth of personality to all mothers, for, like every mother, she gave her Child a name. Since this Child was unique, it was fitting that He be given a name that would describe His Mission. This Child came not to save people from insecurity, or to make them rich and powerful, but to save them from their sins. Hence He was given the name of Jesus, which means Saviour. It was an irreplaceable name, before which the heavens and the earth trembled, and before which our knees bow.

If any one of us could have made our own mother, we

would have made her the most beautiful woman in the world. As God preexisted His Own Mother somewhat in the way that an artist preexists his work, we can understand why she should be the Madonna of the World. Then, when He took on human flesh and became a Babe, we can understand why He climbed up her body as an ivory tower, to kiss upon her lips a Mystic Rose.

The mother is both the physical preserver of life and the moral provider of truth; she is nature's constant challenge to death, the bearer of cosmic plenitude, the herald of eternal realities, God's great cooperator. To this Modern Woman and Pattern Mother, we say in the language of Mary Dixon Thayer:

Lovely Lady dressed in blue—
Teach me how to pray!
God was just your little Boy,
Tell me what to say!
Did you lift Him up, sometimes,
Gently, on your knee?
Did you sing to Him the way
Mother does to me?
Did you hold His hand at night?
Did you ever try
Telling stories of the world?
O! And did He cry?
Do you really think He cares
If I tell Him things—
Little things that happen? And
Do the Angels' wings
Make a noise? And can He hear
Me if I speak low?
Does He understand me now?

Tell me for you know!
Lovely Lady dressed in blue,
Teach me how to pray!
God was just your little Boy,
And you know the way.

CHAPTER SEVEN

# The Philosophy of Communism

Last week, I met a very incredulous gentleman, a taxi driver. After a few blocks he said, "Say, you wouldn't happen to be ——— would you?"

"Yes."

"I wonder how I could ever convince anybody that you were in my cab."

I said, "Come to the office and I will autograph a book for you, and then you can prove it by the autograph."

He said, "They won't believe you autographed it. They will think somebody else did it. Not even my wife will believe me! I want to tell somebody about it while you are on television, but I never get to see you on television. I have to earn my living and every Tuesday night when you are on, I am out hacking."

"Here is five dollars. Next Tuesday night at eight o'clock, you go into a bar, give a dollar of the five to the bartender, and ask him to tune me in on his television set. The four dollars is to pay for not driving your cab that half hour. Then, when we come on the screen, you can tell everyone at the bar."

"Suppose they don't believe me?"

"To overcome that incredulity," I said, "I'll tell you what I will do. Next Tuesday night, I'll tell this story. Then they'll have to believe you."

Now, I have paid my debt.

There is considerable confusion in our American life about Communism; too much emotional hatred of Communism, and not sufficient thinking and reasoning about it.

But Communism is intrinsically wrong, independently of Russia's foreign policy. The foreign policy of Russia is a tactic; it is by the philosophy of Communism that Russia is to be judged.

The two basic principles of Communism which we select for presentation are:

1. Economic determinism.
2. Communist notion of man.

Economic determinism sounds very learned, but it means, very simply, that culture, civilization, religion, philosophy, art, morals, and literature are all *determined* by economic methods of production. The latter is the base on which all else rests.

For example, if the method of production at a given period of history is based on private ownership of property, such as we have here in our democracy, the Communist argues that literature, art, and philosophy are nothing but a superstructure or a defense of private enterprise. "Your literature would be so written," the Communists say, "as to justify slavery, colonialism, capitalism, and the right of property owners to submerge the workers."

"Morals, in like manner," the Communists say, "in private enterprise would be so constructed as to defend ownership." As Lenin wrote, "We deny all morality taken from non-economic class conceptions." Take the seventh and tenth commandments—"Thou shalt not steal" and "Thou shalt not covet thy neighbor's goods." The Communists say, "Can't you see

these two commandments are based upon private property? Why should anyone prohibit stealing except in a society where there is personal ownership of the methods of production? When the state owns everything, there is no need of that morality, for everyone will be so prosperous there will be no need of stealing."

"Religion is based upon the economics of private enterprise, too," contend the Communists. "It is an opiate given to the workers to make them content with being exploited. It leads them to believe that there is another world to make up for all the injustices of this one." The Communists add, "If you change your method of production and, instead of having private enterprise, put all property in the hands of the state, then the superstructure changes. There will then be Communist literature, Communist morals, Communist art, and Communist philosophy."

Communist literature will attack capitalism, make fun of America, and prove that Russia invented everything from flying machines to radar.

Communist morals will see but one wrong, namely, injuring or hurting state property or in any way betraying the revolutionary class.

Art, too, becomes Communistic. During the days when we Americans were foolishly having a honeymoon with Russia, there was a considerable amount of art developed that was Communist-inspired. Remnants of it can be seen in some hotels and public buildings. The art is unmistakable, for it shows great, tremendous, muscular men with little heads (no brains), pushing wheels, pulling at ropes, tugging at plows; *i.e.*, man was made for production; his origin is economic, so is his destiny.

What is the fallacy of economic determinism, which means that economics determines everything? The first fallacy of economic determinism is that Karl Marx, who studied philosophy and should have known better, confused what is known as a *condition* with a *cause*. For example, the window is a *con-*

*dition* of light, but the window is not the *cause* of light. We are willing to admit that economics, to some extent, does condition literature and art. But it certainly does not *cause* literature and art.

If economics is the cause of culture and religion, why, in the pre-Christian era, were different cultures and religions produced by the same economic methods of production? There was no difference between the economic methods of production among the Jews and those among the Hindus or the Chaldeans, but their civilizations were different; their religious and moral concepts were different, the Hebrew having the highest moral concept that was known to man in the pre-Christian era. Since their economic methods of production were identical, it cannot be said that economics was the cause of the differences in cultures.

There was no change of economic methods in the Roman Empire when it became Christian from when it was pagan. But the civilization and the art and the religion and the morality were totally different in the two periods. Therefore, it is not the economics that determines civilization. The way a violin is made does not determine the music that will be played on it.

Economics has gone to the head of the Communists like wine to an empty stomach. Notice that whenever the Communists try to convince us of their superiority, they make moral judgments about us. They say we are "immoral," "unjust," "unethical," and "bad," while they are right and good. These moral judgments do not belong in the economic category. Whence comes their moral worth, if reality be not moral? If economics is at the base of reality, how can it be said that any system is "right" and another "wrong"? If religion be a product of economic method of production, how could it be an opiate? Finally, if changes in morality, art, and culture are due to changes in methods of production, *what causes changes* in the methods of *production?* They are more often due to invention, and invention is an intellectual or a spiritual cause. Those who believe in an ethical order independent of economics can condemn exploitation, but the materialism of Communism cannot do it without repudiating the whole system. They have no right to use the words "right" and "wrong," but only "private" and "social." If everything is economically determined, right and wrong, truth and error have no existence, for they do not fit in an economic category.

Communism is strong only when it borrows some of the moral indignation that has been inherited from the Hebraic-Christian traditions; Communism is weak when it departs from that tradition. Communism has bootlegged and smuggled into its system the decency and morality that have come from the great Hebraic-Christian tradition of the Western world and then uses it to pass judgment on the world. Moral indignation is needed against injustice, but Communists have no basis for using it.

This is a reminder of how we ought to meet Communism on the *Voice of America* and elsewhere, namely, not to talk about the supremacy of our economics. Whenever we talk about the supremacy of economics, we pay tribute to the Communists' error of the primary value of economics. Communists are speaking to the rest of the world on the basis of ethics, which their system repudiates. We, who have moral ideals, are speaking to the rest of the world in terms of economics. They are using the language that we ought to be using.

The second basic principle of Communism is that man has value only inasmuch as he is a member of a class. In one of his earlier writings, Karl Marx, who is the father of Communism, said, "We have already destroyed the outer religion; now we must destroy the inner religion," that is, man's spiritual nature.

Then follows this very remarkable statement in which Marx very correctly tells us the essence of democracy. Marx knew the basis of democracy far better than many who live under its blessings. Marx said that democracy is founded on the principle of the "sovereign worth of a person." "This, in its turn," he continued, "is based upon a postulate, a dream and an illusion of Christianity, namely, that every man has an immortal soul." In the first edition of his work on capital, Marx says, "Persons of and by themselves have no value. An individual has a value only inasmuch as he is the representative of an economic category, 'the revolutionary class'; outside of that, man has no value."

Molotov developed this idea by saying that "bread is a political weapon." We believe in food for the hungry, regardless of who they are. Molotov in good Marxist fashion argues that bread be given only to certain people, namely, those who follow Communist revolutionary ideas.

Some years ago, Heywood Broun told me of a cartoonist employed by one of the Communist papers in New York. The cartoonist developed cancer and was obliged to give up work. Broun went to the Communists and asked if they would not give him some pension to help pay his hospital bills. The answer that he received from the Communists was "He is of no use to us. He is no longer a member of the revolutionary class, and therefore for us he does not exist." That was good Communism, but it is not good humanitarianism. Once you start with the principle that the person has no value, but only the revolutionary class has, then liquidation becomes inevitable.

Man is then likened to lower forms of life in which an individual fly, an individual gnat, an individual ant is of no consequence; what is of importance is the species.

Marx and Communism have turned the supremacy of the species into the supremacy of the class. Once admitted, it follows that what happens to an individual person is of no concern. The revolutionary class of Communism alone has value. Communism is an aggressive religion of the species.

This explains how Russia uses her satellite people in war. Communist tanks run over the bodies of their wounded. No one would even kick them out of the path of the great machines, because they are no longer of worth. It also explains their war tactics in Korea. The first line of attack rushed into battle to be cut down. The second line, which was unarmed, carried mattresses and threw themselves on barbed wire to be shot. The third group had guns and gave battle.

This liquidation of man in the modern world will not be

arrested simply by protests of horror. We must recognize the evil of this Communist philosophy and begin affirming, in the United States, the worth of a person as a creature of God.

As Hitler put the emphasis upon *race*, as Mussolini put it on the *nation*, so the Communists put it on a *revolutionary mass*. The hour has struck to affirm the power and worth and vocation of the individual. That means returning to what Marx rightly saw as the basis of democracy, namely, the truth that every man has an immortal soul. What we are attempting to do now in our Western world is foolishly to preserve the fruits of Christianity without the roots. Personality has a religious basis. A person is a *subject*, not an *object*. A person has more worth than the universe: "What doth it profit a man if he gains the whole world and loses his soul?" A person realizes himself and comes to relative perfection in society, but only because he has within himself a principle independent of a society, namely, a soul. This soul has rights anterior to any state or dictator, parliament or king. As our Declaration of Independence puts it, "The Creator has endowed man with certain inalienable rights." The world must move away from mass civilization by restoring value to the person. The Lord of the Universe saw value in the lowest kind of criminal and addressed him in the second person singular: "This day *Thou* shalt be with Me in Paradise." This promise was the foundation stone of democracy.

Communists are right in saying this world needs a revolution, but not their cheap kind, which merely transfers booty and loot out of one man's pocket into another's. We need the kind of revolution that will purge out of a man's heart pride and covetousness and lust and anger. The true battle against Communism begins in the heart of every single American. The revolution must begin in man before it begins in society. The Communist revolution has been a basic failure; it is not revolutionary enough; it leaves hate in the soul of man. We need not fear Communism as much as we need fear being Godless. If God is with us, then who can be against us?

## CHAPTER EIGHT

# Knowing and Loving

Some probably believe the reason why Cain turned out so badly was because Eve had no books on child psychology.

Those who have read many psychology books have noticed that for the most part they were written for abnormal people. The normal people like yourselves also are entitled to a psychology. When 10,000 run headlong toward an abyss, he who runs from it seems to the others to be in flight. The normal person who refuses to run madly after abnormal psychology may seem to be abnormal, but let him brave the charge.

First, we shall show the difference between knowing and loving, and then the difference between knowing and loving in man and woman.

Our soul has two faculties. One faculty is that of knowing, and the other is the faculty of loving. We are like an animal inasmuch as we have sensations and passions, but knowledge and love are specifically human. Knowing belongs to man's intellect or reason; loving belongs to his will. The object of the intellect is truth; the object of the will is goodness or love.

The intellect and will operate in quite different fashions.

Whenever the intellect knows anything above it in dignity, it always brings the object known *down* to the level of itself. The will, on the contrary, always goes *out* to meet the object loved.

Teachers often have the experience of explaining some abstract principle to children. They do so by bringing the abstract subject down to the level of the child's intellect and his concrete daily experiences. When Divine Wisdom became Man, He taught our poor intellects by parables and similes. When we want to memorize something, we often make an association in our intellect with something we already know. I remember once I was to meet a man by the name of Lummock. My secretary said, "Now, remember that his name rhymes with 'stomach.'" Do you know what I called him? —Kelly!

Why do we say of certain explanations of a subject, "That

is too far above my head"? It is because we cannot understand anything unless it is reduced to the level of our understanding. A teacher who cannot explain any abstract subject to a child does not himself thoroughly understand his subject; if he does not attempt to break down his knowledge to fit the child's mind, he does not understand teaching. It is easier to write a book with footnotes than the same book written so that children can understand it.

Now notice how different the will is. While the intellect brings the thing down to its own level, the will, on the contrary, always goes out to meet the object that it loves. If, for example, you love music, you meet the demands of music and accommodate yourself to its scale and its harmonies. If you love a foreign language, you submit yourself to its grammar and syntax. If a young man is courting a woman who loves poetry, he is very foolish if he talks mathematics.

There is a second difference between the intellect and the will. Whenever the mind or intellect knows anything that is *below* it in dignity, it elevates that thing by knowing it. Whenever mind or intellect knows anything that is *above* it in dignity, to some extent it degrades it.

Birds, flowers, trees, and bugs and all the other objects of physical science are below man in dignity. But when the mind knows these things and draws them into itself, they receive a new kind of existence, a new kind of being. The stone is to some extent "spiritualized" by the mere fact that we know its nature. Aristotle, for that reason, said that the mind of man is a microcosmos—a little universe; it contains the external world within itself and, by doing so, ennobles it. This idea is the basis of the Jewish hymns of praise, such as the Psalms of David or the *Benedicite*. The sun, the sky, the ocean, the mountain, the hail, the rain, the flowers all are called to acknowledge their God through man, who possesses these things within himself by knowledge.

But when we know something that is *above* the mind in dignity, it, to some extent, loses its nobility because we have to pull it down to our level. For example—what does my angel look like? How do you picture an angel? If you draw an angel, you must necessarily make an angel less beautiful than it is. See how feeble the human mind is in dealing with a mystery like the Trinity. When we compare Three Persons in One God to three angles in one triangle, or to ice, water, and steam as three manifestations of the nature of water, we are falling so far below the sublimity of the Godhead that we almost spoil it by describing it.

To describe God, our poor mind is sometimes far more accurate in negating certain imperfections of God than in affirming perfection. That is why we say God is Timeless, Spaceless. The play *The Green Pastures* never attempted to picture God as He is. Hence God was made to appear as a genial, lovable, old colored man. The dramatist knew the mind would spoil Deity by bringing Him down to our level. So by avoiding any attempt at approximation, there was left implied a lovely respect for the Infinite. It is always good theater, for the same reason, never to show the person of Christ on a stage or a screen, because one would miss His Divinity by completely reducing Him to our finite limitations.

The will, on the contrary, when it loves anything above it in dignity, goes out to meet the demands of whatever it loves. When the will loves anything that is below it in dignity, it degrades itself. Suppose the dominant love of man was money. Man would degrade himself by loving what is less worthy than himself. In loving it, he becomes like gold. If a man loves only lust, carnality, and the pleasure of the flesh above all things, he thereby degrades his spirit to the sex level. We become like that which we love. If we love what is base, we become base; but if we love what is noble, we become noble. Hence the importance of the right kind of ideals and the right kind of heroes. As Our Lord said, "Where your treasure is, there is your heart also." Hence the least love of God is worth more than the knowledge of all created things.

Who is our ideal? A player of a percussion instrument, a .398 batter, a soldier, a patriot, a saint? The higher the love, the more demands will be made on us to conform to that ideal. To a great extent the level of any civilization is the level of its womanhood. When a man loves a woman, he has to become worthy of her. The higher her virtue, the more noble her character, the more devoted she is to truth, justice, and goodness, the more a man has to aspire to be worthy of her. The history of civilization could actually be written in terms of the *level of its women.*

The difference between knowing and loving helps solve

the question: Why is it that very learned people are not always religious? The question must not assume that people who are religious are not intellectual. A man can know much and still be evil, because in knowing we bring things to our level, but in loving God we have to go out to His level, and this many so-called "wise" men refuse to do. Knowledge does not necessarily elevate us. A train announcer *knows* all the stations, but he does not travel. A policeman *knows* much about robberies; he *knows* how to get into banks; he *knows* how to break into houses; he may even have a souvenir set of burglar's tools. But he does not rob, because he does not *will* to rob; he does not *love* to be a thief.

Every theologian ought to be a mystic; every D.D., or Doctor of Divinity, ought to be a saint. He *knows* enough to be one; but he does not *will* it, or work hard enough at it. I am a D.D., but I am not a saint. May God have mercy on my soul!

This has been a very abstract lecture so far. Maybe our next point will be more interesting, namely, the difference between a man and a woman in knowing and in loving.

The first difference between a man and a woman is that a man is concerned principally with *things* and a woman with *persons*. Hence a man talks business and a woman of how another woman is dressed. A man's interest is more remote; a woman's interest is more immediate. A man's interest leans to the abstract; a woman's to the concrete and intimate. A man is concerned with ends, goals, and purposes; a woman with something that is very proximate and close and near and dear to her. Because man centers on things and woman on persons, a woman is more inclined to gossip. A woman does not believe everything she hears, but at least she can repeat it.

For example, a man will come home from the office full of business, saying, "Listen, dear, today I got an order for 250,000 nuts and bolts. I was the only firm that could supply them in all Keokuk." His wife will say, "Dear, how do you want your eggs?"

Now, the other way around, to be fair. A man is reading the newspaper. Ever notice that at breakfast he wants to *read*, she wants to *talk?* The wife comes in and says, "Do you notice anything new?" Why is it, after thousands of years of civilization, husbands have never been able to notice new "hair do's" and new hats? I heard of a wife who got even with her husband. He said, "Dear, there's an old-clothesman at the door." She answered, "Tell him I have all I need."

These are differences, but they actually complement one another, and very beautifully. The man is interested in the sowing of wheat in the field; the woman in making the bread. Both the bow and the violin are necessary for good music.

A second difference between the love of a man and the love of a woman is that a man will always give reasons for loving, but a woman gives no reasons for loving.

A man will say, "I love you because you are beautiful; I love you because your teeth are pearly; I love you because you make good shortening bread; I love you because you are sweet."

The woman just says, "I love you." Period.

Man's love is always mixed up with his reasons. Men generally write the love songs. Hence such titles as "That Is

Why I Love You" or reasons like these: "You're the cream in my coffee . . . ," "You're my Shakespeare sonnet . . . , my Mickey Mouse. . . ."

These are not very good reasons for loving, but at least they are reasons. Man's love is always tied up with his intellect; but for a woman, love is its own reason. "I love you because I love you." A man gives reasons because he *compares* one woman with another; a woman just prefers. A man sees one peach in a basket of peaches; a woman sees only the one peach. A father's love for a child varies with the child's obedience to his commands; a mother's love is more immediate and more ready to overlook the faults. If "love is blind," it may be because it gives no reason. But it has a reason, which is choice, election, preference. As Our Lord told His Apostles, "I have *chosen* you."

A woman never tells why she loves; she just tells you *how* she loves. Elizabeth Barrett Browning has given feminine love its best expression in her poem:

> How do I love thee? Let me count the ways.
> I love thee to the depth and breadth and height
> My soul can reach, when feeling out of sight
> For the ends of Being and ideal Grace.
> I love thee to the level of every day's
> Most quiet need, by sun and candlelight.
> I love thee freely, as men strive for Right;
> I love thee purely, as they turn from Praise.
> I love thee with the passion put to use
> In my old griefs, and with my childhood's faith.
> I love thee with a love I seemed to lose
> With my lost saints—I love thee with the breath,
> Smiles, tears of all my life!—and, if God choose,
> I shall but love thee better after death.

A third difference is that defects get in the way of a man's love. But defects never hurt a woman's love. A man hears somebody talk about the woman that he loves or is going to marry, and he will say, "Well, after all, I have got to *know* that woman if I am to marry her; and I had better listen to this."

But a woman won't listen to anybody "running down" her intended. She knows the man has defects, but she loves him anyway. Her attitude is that of the popular song, "He's Just My Bill." He may be a good-for-nothing blankety-blank-blank, but he's my Bill, anyway. A man's love decreases with the revelation of defects; a woman's does not. A woman gets angry when a man denies his faults, because she knew them all along. His lying mocks her affection; it is the deceit that angers her more than the faults.

There is something divine in that kind of love, because God loves us in spite of all defects, our failings, and our sins. A man may stand for the Justice of God, but a woman stands for His Mercy.

To summarize, notice two steps in the relation of knowing and loving. At the beginning we never can love anybody or anything unless we *know* that person or *know* that thing. That is why there has to be an introduction to a person before there can be the beginning of love for that person. Then, after a time, we come to the second step: *love creates knowledge*. How often that happens, for example, in an enduring marriage between a husband and wife. They know one another's moods, attitudes, fears, joys, without ever a word being spoken. They have loved one another so deeply they have created a new kind of knowledge.

In order to love God, we must know Him. But by loving Him, we increase our understanding of Him. Our Lord said that if we obeyed His commandments, that is, loved Him, we would *know* His doctrine.

A French infidel once said to Pascal, "If I had your brains, I would be a better man." Pascal answered, "Be a better man, and you will have my brains." The cause of a wrong *mental* state is often a wrong *moral* state. Our brains today are big enough. Could it be that our hearts are too small?

## CHAPTER NINE

# Conscience

There has been a poll taken concerning our television show, and no one in a certain category listens to it.

Remember the story of the taxi driver a few weeks ago, to whom I offered five dollars to make up for the time lost while he tipped some bartender in order that he might tune us in on TV? I just received this tragic letter from the taxi driver:

"It was 7:45 P.M. and I was on Times Square, when a man got into the cab and said, 'Cortlandt Street.' Knowing I had fifteen minutes until you would be on TV, I stepped on the gas and got there about three minutes to eight.

"I stopped the cab, went into the first bar, and had a beer. [What a moment this is for a commercial!] They had Milton Berle on and the place was crowded. I left there, went across the street to another bar, and they had Berle on. I jumped into my cab, went to another bar, ordered a beer, and they had Berle on. I went to another, they had Berle on. So I left and kept on walking, until I reached West Street on the waterfront, and I noticed a bar on the corner. I could see the bar and one lonely customer from the outside, and I could see the screen of the TV set was not on.

"I said to myself, 'I can't miss now.' I walked in, had a beer and kindly asked the bartender would he put you on. He started to swear; the TV set was out of order. I felt kind of blue by then, for it was twenty-eight minutes after eight, so I gave up.

"I went home and ate, and continued to work."

Not one television set were we on, *bar none*.

A number of clippings came from Chicago. It seems that within the last few weeks, the Murphy family was watching TV upstairs. A robber came in and took about three hundred dollars in cash and a couple of thousand dollars in jewels.

The next day one of the robbers phoned and said, "We found out that we were in the wrong house. We are very sorry; we sure did have butterflies in our stomach when we saw Bishop Sheen on television."

Apparently, that is the only effect we have—we create butterflies in stomachs. We apparently did not disturb their consciences or induce them to return the stolen goods.

For that reason the subject of this telecast will be—conscience.

What is conscience? Conscience is a judgment of our reason telling us that we ought to do good and avoid evil. That brings up the question: What makes anything "good"? A thing is good if it attains the end and the highest purpose for which it is made. A pencil is good if it writes, for that is the purpose of a pencil. But the pencil is not "good" to open a can with, for it was not made to open cans. If we use a pencil to open a can, not only do we not open it, but we break the pencil. If we use our lives for other purposes than those given by God, not only do we miss happiness, but we actually hurt ourselves and beget in us queer little "kinks."

Are these *good* television cameras that stare us in the face? Some might say, "Yes, they are good television cameras because the men that run them have little saddles on which to sit, and one union man pushes around another union man." Others might say, "A television camera is good because it tests the composure and the poise of anyone on the stage; they sneak up on you and try to distract you, if possible." But these are not the reasons why a television camera was invented. The purpose of a camera is rather to record images and then transmit them to your set. The television camera is "good" if it does that.

Apply that to man. When is man "good"? A man is good when he attains the highest purpose for which he was made. This supreme goal cannot be to get the maximum of pleasure out of this life, because those who concentrate on having a good time rarely have it. Pleasure is only a bonus or a by-product of a duty. One does not eat ice cream to have pleasure; one has pleasure because one eats ice cream. If we set our affections not, say, on the family but on the pleasure a man hopes to have from having a family, the pleasure vanishes. Furthermore, our experience proves that we are most happy when we do not seek our own pleasure at all; the glutted, the jaded, the satiated are more miserable than the man who lives to serve his neighbor.

Fame, reputation, a full safety-deposit vault cannot be the

supreme goal of life either, because all these things are extrinsic to man; it matters little how much one has on the *outside* if he is not happy on the inside.

If man is to be perfectly happy, he must have *Life, Truth,* and *Love.* Not life for five minutes, but Life without age or decay, a Life in which one possesses at each and every moment the fullness of all joys; this means eternal Life, for so long as we are in time, one joy excludes another, *e.g.*, the joy of dining with Shakespeare and Homer. Happiness demands "everything at once." But we also need Truth, or the full ocean of Knowledge and Wisdom. Finally, to be happy, we need Love, not a love that turns to hate, not a love we become used to or a love that makes us "fed up," but an abiding ecstasy of Love. This Perfect Life, Perfect Truth, and Perfect Love is God. It is the Infinite God we need to satisfy the infinite cravings of our heart. It was for Him we were made and "our hearts are restless until they rest in Him."

Now we are in a position to answer in a simple fashion what is "good" and "bad." Anything is good which brings us close to this Life, Truth, and Love; anything is bad which detours us from that goal. Obviously what is good for a pig is not good for a man. Each thing must be judged by its nature, and the nature of a man is quite different from the nature of a monkey.

Everything in the universe has something implanted in its nature by God to make it attain the purpose for which it was created. Chemicals combine in exactly the same way everywhere in the universe, because God gave to each of them its own atomic weight and power to combine with or replace other elements. Scientists discovered this law put there by the Creator and named it the "law of valence."

The plant kingdom has another kind of law, which, for example, makes an acorn turn into an oak, as if there were a little architect working on the inside of it. Biology discovered these God-given laws and called them the "laws of metabolism."

Animals, in order to attain the end for which they were made, have instincts. All these things execute the Divine Will without knowing why and without being able not to do it.

But, when you come to man, there is *reason* and *will* by which man can think out his final goal and also can freely will to follow it or reject it.

The lower orders *must* be what they are. A primrose can never be a tomcat, but man has no "must" imposed upon him; having an intellect and free will, man merely *ought* to do something. That "oughtness" is recorded in conscience.

Each of us has the power to regulate something *outside* of us, *e.g.*, to throw a shoe at a screeching cat at midnight. But we also have the power to regulate something *inside* us, namely, to determine our character. Many things *happen to us*, but what is more important is what we *make happen to ourselves*. We are self-determining creatures, unlike frogs and stones.

Everyone appeals to a standard of conduct, even though he denies it. Half man's life is spent in telling himself what he "ought" to do or his neighbor what he "ought" to do. Ants never say, "Get in line"; pigs at a trough never say, "Wait your turn"; bears never growl to other bears, "You would not want me to do that to you." Only humans use the argument, "Yes, but I saw it first." There is no sense in saying anything is wrong, unless we know what is right. No referee could call a foul in basketball games unless there were rules.

This "oughtness" in us, which is not mechanical, or biological, or instinctive, but rational, implies a standard. Conscience puts before us certain principles to guide our actions. Conscience itself needs help, but we are not going to discuss that here. We are all born with the power of speech, but we need grammar. Conscience, too, needs Revelation.

(We will tell you what conscience is, if our little angel will let us use the blackboard. Did you know that, in Heaven, an angel is a no-body?)

Our conscience is very much like the best government in the world, that is to say, the government of the United States. Our government has three functions and branches:

Modern science has explored the whole surface of the earth, made the sea reveal the secrets of its depths, the sun tell the story of its wanderings, and the stars the mystery of their light—but all this exploration is external. Modern man has done little to explore that region which is nearest to him, and yet most unknown, namely, the depths of his own conscience.

What is conscience? Conscience is an interior government, exercising the same functions as all human government, namely, legislative, executive, and judicial. It has its Congress, its President, and its Supreme Court: it makes its laws, it witnesses our actions in relation to the laws, and finally it judges us.

First, conscience legislates. One needs only to live to know that there is in each of us an interior Sinai, from which is promulgated, amid the thunder and lightning of daily life, a law telling us to do good and avoid evil. Without even being consulted, conscience plays its legislative role, pronouncing some actions to be in themselves evil and unjust and others in themselves moral and good.

Second, conscience not only is legislative, in the sense that it lays down a law, but it is also executive, in the sense that it witnesses the application of the law to actions. An imperfect, but helpful, analogy is to be found in our own government. Congress passes a law, then the President witnesses and approves it, thus applying the law to the lives of citizens. In like manner, conscience executes laws in the sense that it witnesses the fidelity of our actions to the law. Aided by memory, it tells us the value of our actions, tells us if we were total masters of ourselves, how much passion, environment, force, and fury influence us; whether our consequences were foreseen or unforeseen; shows us, as in a mirror, the footsteps of all our actions; points its finger at the vestiges of our decisions; comes to us as a true witness and says, "I was there, I saw you do it. You had such and such an intention." In the administration of human justice the law can call together only those witnesses who have known me externally, but conscience as a witness summons not only those who saw me but summons *me who know myself*. And whether I like it or not, I cannot lie to what it witnesses against me.

Finally, conscience not only lays down laws, not only witnesses my obedience or disobedience to them, but it also judges me accordingly. The breast of every man bears a silent court of justice. Conscience is the judge, sitting in judgment, handing down decisions with such authority as to admit of no appeal, for no one can appeal a judgment which he brings against himself. That is why there gather about the bar of conscience all the feelings and emotions associated with right and wrong —joy and sorrow, peace and remorse, self-approval and fear, praise and blame. If I do wrong, it fills me with a sense of guilt from which there is no escape; if the inmost sanctuary of my being is assaulted by the stern voice of this judge, I am driven out of myself by myself. Whence, then, can I fly but to myself with the sickening sense of guilt, remorse, and disgrace, which is the very hell of the soul? If, on the contrary, conscience approves my action, then there settles upon me, like the quiet of an evening dew, the joy which is a stranger to the passing pleasures of sense.

Thus it is that by turning the searchlight into the hidden recesses, I find that my conscience reveals itself as making laws, witnessing my obedience to them, and finally as passing on them judgments of praise and blame, innocence and guilt. Manifestly, this triple role, upon the model of which all human government is based, must have a reason for its order. But where seek it?

What is the source of the legislative, executive, and judicial role of my conscience? It does not come from myself, for no one can be his own legislator and a superior to himself. Furthermore, if the law of conscience were of my own making, I could unmake it; but I cannot do this, for it comes to me in defiance of my own will. When my will is set against hearing it, or even obeying it, it comes as a delegate with absolute right to rule over me. This means that I did not make it but that I am free only to obey it or to disobey it.

Neither does it come from society, for society is merely an interpreter of the law of conscience and not its author. Human laws may sanction it and elaborate it, but they do not create it. The approval or disapproval of society did not make the right and wrong of my conscience, because sometimes conscience bids us to flout the laws of society, when they are inimical to the laws of God, as was the case with the martyrs who died for the Faith.

If, therefore, the voice of that interior Sinai of conscience is neither from me nor from society, and if it is universal in its whisperings and articulations, so that no moral creature can wholly shake it off, it must be that behind this law there is a Lawmaker, and behind this voice there is a Person, and behind this command a Power, which is God. He has sealed upon every man coming into the world the light which illumines souls in the paths of peace to the homeland of the children of liberty.

Thus an examination of my conscience and its triple role forces me to conclude that just as the eye corresponds to things visible, the ear to things audible, reason to things intelligible, so, too, the law of my conscience ought to correspond to a Power which legislates, the witness of my conscience must correspond to a Righteousness which executes, and the praise and blame of my conscience to a Justice which judges. Since Power,

Righteousness, and Justice correspond to the essential attributes of a Person, I must conclude that that Personal Power is Intelligent in order to make laws; that the Personal Righteousness is All-Knowing, in order to have a perfect insight into moral character; and that that Personal Justice is Supreme, in order to pass sentences after His judgments. And that Wise Power, All-Knowing Righteousness, and Supreme Justice, before Whom I kneel in sorrow, is God.

It may be objected, "If God knows what I am going to do, if He knows that I would rob and steal, why did He create me?"

The answer is, "God did not make you as a creature that steals and robs. You made yourself as a thief and a robber." We are self-creating beings; we have the power within ourselves to choose our actions. This involves self-determination. Those who say we create "complexes" by resisting our lower nature forget that a complex is not set up by resisting a temptation, but rather by yielding to it. We are not only in this world as *objects*—that is to say, things do not only happen to us; we are also *subjects* in the sense that we make things happen. Every one of our free choices forms a pattern in our lives; this pattern is our character.

Everything we do, whether good or evil, goes down into our unconscious mind. At the end of the day, the businessman will pull out of his cash register all the debits and credits of the day. So at the end of every human life there will be pulled out of our subconscious or unconscious mind the record of every thought, word, and deed. This will be the basis of our judgment.

Consider briefly psychiatry and conscience. In order to understand the relation of psychiatry to conscience, it is well to recall that every act may be considered from two points of view: (1) as an act of the will; (2) as an act involving our psychological make-up, our impulses, instincts, habits, and character. Human freedom always passes through our body, through our brain, through our character—whatever that happens to be—and these are not the same in all individuals. In some individuals the psychological make-up is normal, and in other individuals it is abnormal.

The will is to be likened to water in a reservoir; the psychological personality through which the act of choice passes into action is likened to the pipes or conduits.

The act of the will also may be likened to an electrical dynamo; the psychological personality to the wiring in our house. Sometimes, the wires get all crossed up and cause a short circuit. These correspond to mental kinks and psychoses.

For example, it is normal for a person freely to love animals; it is abnormal to keep two hundred cats in a living room. I heard of a woman who had seven cats. She had seven holes cut in every door in the house. Asked the reason, she said, "When I say 'Scat!' *I mean it.*"

A man chooses to go hunting. That is a very normal decision and a free act at a certain time of the year. That decision passes into act according to his mental or physical disposition, and he decides *what* he will shoot, *where* he will shoot and the *animal* he will shoot. To decide to hunt bears in a certain locality would be normal. Now, suppose he takes his gun, and instead of gunning for bears he guns for a mother-in-law. That is abnormal; it is *very* abnormal.

Where does psychiatry belong at this point? Psychiatry belongs to the area of the abnormal psychological make-up in the diagram. Psychiatry takes care of abnormal releases of free decision, or the "short circuits."

The normal releases belong to the domain of psychology, while free choice belongs to the domain of philosophy and morals.

What will a psychiatrist do when he finds someone who abnormally expresses himself by gunning for his mother-in-law? He will make use of an age-old method of analyzing motivation. He will say, "Now, I want to go down into your subconscious mind and bring to the level of consciousness, if it is at all possible, certain feelings, ideas, and emotions which you may have had in the past, and which have become so crossed up that now you want to shoot your mother-in-law." The psychiatrist might ask, "Did anyone ever compare your mother-in-law to an animal?" "Yes," he said, "some call her an 'old bear.' " That mental association caused the abnormal act of gunning for a mother-in-law. The psychiatrist is now in a position to straighten out his mind after bringing the "crossed wires" to the surface.

In dealing with human minds, two mistakes must be avoided. One mistake would be for the psychiatrist to say there is no such thing as human guilt because there is only disease and abnormality. The other mistake would be for the psychologist, or the philosopher or the moralist, to say that all physical and psychical factors can be ignored in judging morality. When the moralist gets into the abnormal where psychiatry belongs and denies the necessity of psychiatry, he is out of his field. When the psychiatrist denies freedom, responsibility, guilt and says that we are all sex-determined, he is out of his field. Disease is one thing; guilt another. When the two are together, the psychiatrist and the moralist work together. A democracy is a government based on personal responsibility. We must never interpret emancipation as an evasion of responsibility, nor think that a responsibility is a hindrance to freedom; rather it is its safeguard.

We have formed, and we must continue to form, associations to safeguard freedom, but let us also persuade Americans to form associations which will safeguard our responsibilities. The bane of democracy is the flight from responsibility on which freedom rests. If America is to continue to be great along the tradition of her Founding Fathers and not betray the Christian traditions, her citizens must release not their evil inclinations from within but rather the aspiration for total goodness that God put in their hearts.

## CHAPTER TEN

# "For Better or Worse"

I wonder why Cupid is always presented as so young? Is it because love never grows up, or because its ideal is always to be young and fresh? Why does he have an arrow? Maybe it is because love is something that wounds and implies sacrifice for others. In any case, in this telecast, we shall discuss, first, some tensions that are common to all marriages, and then some problems that are peculiar to certain marriages.

There are three tensions in married love. By tensions, we mean emotions which pull in opposite directions, like a tug of war. There is nothing wrong about them. They are common, in a certain sense, not only to the love of a husband and wife, but to human existence and even to the love of souls for God.

1. The tension of unity and separateness.
2. The tension of the personal and the social.
3. The tension of longing and satiety.

It is the nature of all love to desire to become one with that which is loved. God loves man. God became man and appeared in the habit and form of man, as Jesus Christ. There is something about all human affection which wants the "I" to be absorbed in another. True love is born of both a need and an emptiness which urge the hunger to be satisfied at the storehouse of another. This need is a proof of our creatureliness and of our basic need for God.

But while this craving for unity is essential to all love, nevertheless there is also bound up with it a tremendous amount of separateness. Sometimes at the moment of the greatest unity, there can be a consciousness of the greatest separateness. A person can be rudely thrown back on himself, even when he most seeks to lose himself in another. This is particularly true where there is body-love and not soul-love. Personality seeks to surrender and yet finds itself back on its own hands. This tension between wanting to lose self and at the same time being confronted with self exists also in the spiritual realm. I once asked a monk what was the greatest trial in the monastery. I thought he would say fasting, penance, long vigils. He said, "No, each of us wants to be united with God, and yet we find that we are not united with Him in the way we want, because of our own imperfection, and our weak human nature—this constitutes our greatest trial."

Coming back to the love of human beings, the reason why there is separateness despite the craving for unity is because we are composed of body and soul. Each person is a world made up of matter and spirit—not that matter and spirit are divided in us, because the soul infuses the *whole* body. But one person is unable to be completely united with another because *matter is the basis of impenetrability or division; spirit is the basis of unity*. We come close to unity because of our spirit; we are precluded from it because we are physical as well as spiritual beings. This does not mean to say that body-love is incompatible with soul-love, for in marriage the first is the condition of the second. It only means that the ideal unity which body-love seeks to attain never is completely realized as an abiding and permanent thing.

A piece of chalk cannot be one with a blackboard because they are both material. Notice how different it is in the case of learning a poem by heart. Because you learn the soliloquy of Hamlet by heart does not preclude me or anyone else from learning it. In fact, the more of us who know the poem, the more we are united with one another. The spirit unites; matter divides. Because an apple is material, it can be divided; but an act of faith cannot be divided. Faith unites people, but economic goods become the subject of quarrels.

In marriage the more emphasis is upon the material, the corporal, or the body, the less is the unity of soul. The reason why our soul is not completely satisfied with human love here below is not due so much to others, as to our failure to understand human nature. Love does not fail; we fail to understand love.

(While my angel is cleaning the blackboard, may I recall to your mind the remark of the man who said he was married to an angel because his wife was always flitting about, was constantly "up in the air," and she never had anything to wear?)

The second tension is between the personal and the social. Love, by its very nature, is personal. "Two is company, three is a crowd." Sex is replaceable, but love is not, because love is always directed to a particular person. No one in all the world, for example, can take the place of a mother. The ideal, in love, is where the "I" and the "Thou" approach one another as if there were no one else in all the world. Personal love resents intrusion; the very absence of the other person causes loneliness and emptiness.

Notice the tension. Though love of husband and wife is personal, it nevertheless by its very nature ends in something social, namely, the family. It is not that the raising of a family spoils personal love; rather is it true that the raising of a family is a proof of the mutual love of husband and wife. All we want to indicate is that in married love there is something *personal*, something *social*. The personal is the deliberate will to love the other; the social is that side of the body-unity which is automatic and of a reflex nature and which to some extent is outside personal control. It is this reflex character of body-love which indicates that God has a hand in every personal love, for by it he preserves the human race.

This relationship of the personal and the social could be illustrated in the chemical order. It is a fact that hydrogen "goes around" a great deal with oxygen. Hydrogen would like to be alone with oxygen, and oxygen with hydrogen. They run around together, and what happens? $H_2O$, or water.

Water is different from hydrogen and oxygen in isolation. Husband and wife, in their love for one another, find that they are drawn to create something greater than themselves, which is the incarnation of their mutual love.

A third tension is between longing and satisfaction. All the poetry of love is a cry and a moan, because everyone recognizes his finiteness and yearns to overcome that imperfection in someone outside himself.

But along with longing, there is satiety and satisfaction. Human beings oscillate between being loved too little and being loved too much; they feel a tug of war between wanting human affection and not wanting it. We have our feet in mud and our wings in the skies. You pick up a cat, the cat wants to be petted, and it purrs. At another time, it will scratch your eyes out. I always like the little girl who said one day to her mother, when the cat was purring, "The cat went to sleep and left its engine running."

This tension may be likened to the boy who asked his mother for a third dish of ice cream; the mother, on discovering he couldn't eat it, said, "See, too much ice cream." He said, "No, not enough boy."

We are not wrong in wanting perfect love. But it so happens that our souls and our hearts are not big enough; thus there is this pull between the two. Jimmy Durante put this thought into a song. I shall be one man who will not attempt to imitate the inimitable. I will merely tell you what Jimmy does. Remember, Jimmy starts to go out the door; he takes off his hat, puts it back on again; takes off his coat, and puts it back on again. Then he says, "Did you ever get the feeling that you wanted to go? And still you got the feeling that you wanted to stay?" That is the way it is with the human heart.

Put these three tensions together and what is the answer? Some would say life is a snare and an illusion, promising what it cannot deliver. They then immerse themselves in adding one finite pleasure to another, mostly carnal, in the hope of reaching the infinite. But they are doomed to failure, for all they are doing is adding zeros. In vain will any man think he will produce the best melody by picking up a succession of violins.

Love that always seems to seek its own pleasure is never really satisfied with the love that it gets. What often was the "ideal woman" or the "ideal man" at the beginning becomes "a bore" within eighteen months. The penalty for selfishness in love is terrific. In egotistical love, the ego, or self, is projected into the other, not to love the other, but to love the self and its pleasures immersed in the other. A man enlarges his ego in the object he loves and thus flatters himself that he is loving another; it is actually his own ego he loves. What seems like love is sterility trying to find happiness in a seeming consecration to others. Love then degenerates into an epidermic contact or a mutual exchange of egotisms, where there is external contact like that of billiard balls, but no true affection. Such love becomes like the relation between a driver of an automobile and the seller of gas on the highway. The other is loved only because of the pleasure or service which he or she gives, but not because of the person independently of the pleasure.

These tensions in marriage can be reduced to the tension of the capture and the chase. There is great joy in the chase, and there is great joy in the killing of the game. There is a thrill in romance and courtship. There is a thrill in marriage. Marriage often kills the romance, and romance extended too long may kill the marriage. To be happy there ought to be the union of both the capture and the chase in such a way that one would never spoil the other.

This tension will be solved only in heaven. Once we *capture* God through a good life on this earth, we shall possess the Infinite which our heart so ardently craves. But it will take an eternity of *chase* to sound the depths of Divine Love. Then the chase and the capture will be one. All that these tensions mean is that here on earth we have the spark, there we shall have the Flame; here we enjoy the sunbeam, there, the Sun; here, the fleeting stream, there, the Ocean of Love. On this earth we have merely a note; the melody is beyond. In the meantime, we must be assured that all of the words of love cannot be written on the cover of a book of this life.

Now we come to difficulties peculiar to some marriages. For example, there is a marriage in which the husband may be an alcoholic or the wife a spendthrift, or the husband unfaithful or the wife always nagging, or he is a "beast" or she is "impossible."

What is going to be done in a case like that? *Stick it out!* Remain faithful! Why? Suppose the husband, instead of being an alcoholic, had pneumonia. Would the wife nurse him and care for him? If he is a sinner he has moral pneumonia and is spiritually sick; why abandon him? A mother has a child with polio; does she give up the child? St. Paul tells us that "the believing wife sanctifieth the unbelieving husband; the believing husband sanctifieth the unbelieving wife." There can be a transfusion of power from one to the other. Sometimes the condition of making the other better is perseverance and love.

A young German girl, at the close of the last World War, who was very learned and had read Homer at seventeen, was courted by one of our American GIs in Berlin. She married him, and they came to this country, where she discovered that he wanted only to read Western stories while frequenting saloons and refused to work. While supporting both of them, she wrote to me, saying, "I was thinking of divorce, but I know that if I divorce him, I am contributing to the ruin of civilization. It does not mean very much if I pull my own individual finger out of that dam; just a little water will come through. But if every woman in the world in a similar situation does the same, then the floodtides will sweep over the world. So I am going to stick it out; but I cannot do so without faith, and you must help me to get it." We gave her instructions, and God gave her the gift of faith. The husband is now an officer in the Army, a different kind of man, and both are raising a fine family.

Certain things which we have in us, once they are given out, are never meant to be taken back. One is the air we breathe; if we take that air back upon ourselves, it poisons us. Love is another. When love is breathed out to another human heart, it is never meant to be taken back. If it is taken back, it suffocates and poisons us.

It may well be that the sacrificial devotion of a wife in such an hour of crisis is the condition of the husband's recovery. Where fleshly love may not heal, sacrificial love may well work the miracle. All suffering endured with love of God profits our families and even the world. Where there is alcoholism, disgruntled tempers, the burdens of others become as impediments to one's own happiness, but where there is true charity, they become as opportunities for service. When carnal love breaks down, then Christian love must step into the breach. The other person is then regarded not as the condition of one's *happiness* but as the condition of one's *salvation*.

Many a marriage may be a living martyrdom, but at least the one who practices it can be sure that he is not robbing his own soul of honor and fidelity. Why should we expect our soldiers to be faithful to their country in the muck and mire, when the husbands and wives desert the cause at the first bursting of a shell? A soldier when drafted does not accept the sentence of death, but he is prepared to face death rather than lose honor. An unhappy marriage is not a condemnation to misery; it is a courageous bearing of the burdens of another rather than denying the vow to "Love until death do us part."

It is not so much the trials and sufferings in certain marriages that make the marriage unbearable; it is how we *react* to the sufferings. If the trial is regarded as the canceling out of the ego and its pleasures, it begets an inferno within; if it is regarded as permitted by God for a greater good, it can positively create an inner joy. When either husband or wife gives up because of the trial, there is just that much less love and heroism in the world. The refusal to love is hell. Though love is not returned, this is no reason for not loving. Rather it is reason for loving: "You love those who love you. What reward is there in this?" But to go on loving in the midst of hate, to sow seeds of kindness where there is no hope of harvest, to forgive when hands are being pierced with nails is not only to diminish the hate of others by localizing marital infections and thus preventing them from becoming epidemics; it is also to purchase the recovery of others through love, for some souls can be purchased only by sacrifice. The government does not abandon soldiers on battlefields because they can no longer fight; fathers do not disown their sons because they have a period of foolish immaturity. In each case, there is respect for the other, because the other is a *person* having value in himself independently of whether he earns or fights, or does not earn. Let there be in the home a respect for the partner, not on the basis of whether the partner gives pleasure, but because the partner is a person, and a gift of God to be loved as one's own flesh. Then there will be less cowardice and surrender, more courage and more faith and a better America. But to love another for God's sake, we must really believe in God.

## CHAPTER ELEVEN

# Teen-Agers

The best definition of an adult that was ever given is one who has stopped growing at both ends and has begun to grow in the middle. But no one has ever given a good definition of a teen-ager.

George Bernard Shaw once said, "It is a pity that youth has been wasted on the young." The contrary is true. It is no secret at all that the Good Lord knew that it was better to put the illusions of life at the beginning in order that as we grew closer to eternity, we might the better see the purpose of living.

Since we cannot think of a good definition of a teen-ager, possibly it would be interesting to discuss the psychology of the teen-ager. The psychology of teen-agers may be reduced to three dominant characteristics: self-consciousness, imitativeness, and restlessness.

The difference between a child and a teen-ager is that a child wants to be loved, a teen-ager wants to love. The affections of free choice are preferred to the natural affections in the family.

When a teen-ager emerges, he discovers his own personality and begins to affirm his ego. A teen-ager is like a chick just breaking the shell in which he has been confined—the shell of the family—and beginning to find himself in a great, broad world. Identification bracelets begin to appear: "It's me!" Up to this point, his life has been merged very much in the family. If the parents say, "We are going to visit Aunt Jane

today," the child has to go. But the teen-ager puts up an argument; he refuses to be a part of an anonymous group. His personality asserts itself, saying, "I don't want to go." This is the age when the boy begins to carry a comb, and the girl wins the battle of lipstick. The only world in which they feel at home is with fellow teen-agers. Hence they have a language of their own. Only in their own milieu do they feel they are understood. They are rather proud of it when nobody understands them. Ordinary words have little "exchange value," particularly with adults. There is much they would have to say if they could find words. Fear of being misunderstood drives them to silence or else to "bebop talk," which only the initiated can understand.

In addition to that, they love to wear clothes that attract attention. They feel that there is a kind of conspiracy against their own ego which they resist by overasserting themselves. The boys wear socks that are so "loud" their feet can never go to sleep. Girls do their hair a thousand different ways to express various personalities. There is a fondness for writing names on fences, driving hot rods, making loud noises on street corners and in busses, in order that people may be conscious that here, at last, a personality is beginning to emerge.

Gestures are quick, gauche, and awkward. Sloppiness is cultivated to attract attention; feelings are easily hurt. But all these are signs that a personality is being born into the adult world, and democracy is founded on personalities. Be not too hard on them.

The second characteristic of a teen-ager is imitation. The ego must emerge from its interiority. It may do it in one of two ways, either by *creation* or by *imitation*. If the teen-ager is keen on developing his own character, being himself and not someone else, then he creates; he assumes responsibility; he has a sense of value, and he discovers the purpose of life and concentrates on the development of his character in a constructive way. He is willing to say "No" to certain things; he resists the crowd and the mob, knowing that the crowd and the mob are often wrong. There are not many, however, who are creative, even among adults. The creative group in society is always the minority.

Release from inferiority most often comes through imitation. Imitation is an escape from responsibility, the ignoring of character building, a flight from true self-expression, and the avoidance of originality. Imitation enables the ego to assert without being committed to moral values or self-restraint. The teen-ager then becomes very sensitive to outside influences and is afraid of ever doing anything which is not "the thing." A teen-ager in such a case never really becomes *himself* or *herself*, but *like* others. He imitates to escape choosing in such a way as to develop personal responsibility. Imitation without moral standards is loss of personality or the spoiling of character. This kind of mimicry develops a mass civilization which is the raw material of Communism.

Imitation is seen in boys who want to be like the "old man"; so they smoke. Some of them even inhale! Some boys even smoke pipes to look like authors! They are the more "studious" kind. Girls wear high heels and, whenever possible, Mother's mink. Father still owes eight hundred dollars on it, but they want it. Ever notice, when a high school empties, that almost all girls are dressed alike? A few dress a certain way, and almost everyone follows.

Because this is the age when personality is not able to stand by itself, it loves to merge into groups and fan clubs; there is even a kind of mass courtship, in which a group of boys will meet a group of girls—they find it difficult to present their own personalities to each other. Hardly strong enough to stand on his own amorous feet, a youth has to lean on somebody else. Hero worship is very strong; very often the hero is a player of the drums, or a celluloid phantom, or a moaning singer. The nobler the hero, the nobler the character which will unfold in later life.

Sometimes the teen-ager revolts against the parents, because he feels that this personality of his should not be submerged in another. He forgets very often that the parents were once teen-agers and hence know the strength and weakness of those difficult years. Parents have greater vision and are capable of better guidance than youth suspects.

The third characteristic of a teen-ager is restlessness. The teen-ager is like mercury, which can be dispersed in several directions. The restlessness is due in part to the discovery of vital and biological impulses stirring within. The body-imperative is more immediate than the soul-imperative. Hence the teen-ager finds perseverance difficult and long attention to the same subject almost impossible. It is this fidgety quality which most tries the patience of adults. He discovers less the laws than the illusions of life. This tremendous physical energy is ready to spend itself on a tackling dummy or "jitterbugging" but almost completely disappears when Mother wants the screens put up in the springtime. "Puppy love," "crushes," and infatuations are common. There are no friendships that seem closer than the friendships of teen-agers, and yet there are hardly any friendships that are quite as volatile. Adults must remember, however, that this urge for affection, for love, for friendship, for society, is good and right. God put it in them, and it is not to be crushed, but developed along right lines.

There are various kinds of music: there is *head* music, such as the music of Bach; there is *heart* music, like Schubert's; and then there is what might be called *visceral* music, that is, music which stirs legs, arms, and the body in general. Teen-agers generally love that kind of music. It is a music in which there is the suggestion of movement, but since the notes are not carried through, the listener is induced to complete the motion. That is why it comes out in violent antics, giving a release to the tremendous biological pressure within. Swooning often accompanies it as the consummation of an emotion. "Swooning" is a vicarious, erotic experience, a desire to live out to the utmost the emotions generated within. General MacArthur said that old soldiers never die, they just fade away; so do teen-agers fade away.

The great advantage of mercurial restlessness is the fact that the young are able to exhaust many of the possible vocations that there are in life. In this time of life, the teen-ager decides for himself whether he will be a lawyer, a doctor, a farmer, or a professor. In his drive from one task to another he often finds his life career.

We have noted three characteristics of teen-agers. The first two are psychical, and the third, which is biological, deserves further stress. Here we shall speak of a virtue which is hardly ever held up to teen-agers, a virtue which is the key to their future happiness and good social relations, the virtue of purity.

Too often, it is thought that this virtue is negative, the denial of self-expression, the extinction of personality, the suppression of vital urges. It is none of these things; it is something very positive. Pure water is more than the absence of dirt; a pure diamond is more than the absence of carbon; purity has its own content.

What is purity? *Purity is reverence for mystery.* Mystery, like a sacrament, is made up of two elements; one is visible, and the other is invisible; one is material, and the other ethereal. A handshake is a mystery or a sacrament; there is something visible about it, namely, the clasping of hands; there is something invisible and spiritual too, namely, the communication of friendship. A word is mystery. There is something material about it, namely, the auditory stimuli or the sound. The horse hears a joke as much as you do, but the horse does not give a horselaugh, and you do. Why? Because the horse does not have the capacity and the power to understand the invisible spiritual element, namely, the meaning of words. A kiss is a mystery. There is something visible or material, such as the touching of lips; the invisible, spiritual element is the communication of affection. When the spiritual element is wanting, it becomes an insult.

Purity is a reverence for mystery. What mystery? The mystery of sex. Sex has two elements. One is material—everyone is male or female. The other is spiritual, namely, the power of creativeness that has been given to man and woman. Almighty God has prolonged His great creative power to man and woman. It is this urge for creativeness that drives man and woman to marry and then stirs them to bring forth the mutual incarnation of their love, or the raw material for the Kingdom of Heaven.

So sacred has been this consciousness of the power of creativity, that all people, Jewish, Christian, and pagan, have always surrounded marriage with religious, sacred, liturgical rites in order to indicate that here is the communication of a great God-given power.

*Purity is reverence for the mystery of creation.* Why is it no one is ever scandalized at seeing people eat in public? There are some who do not mind eating in the front window of Child's on Fifth Avenue in New York. Most people in Paris eat outside. But why is it that we are scandalized by seeing people make love in public? Is a manifestation of affection wrong? Certainly not! Why then are we shocked? We are shocked because there is something so personal, so intimate, so sacred and mysterious about love that we do not want to see it vulgarized, profaned, and made common.

Obscenity is the turning of mystery into a jest. It is the making of something holy, unholy, and something personal, vulgar. Vulgar comes from the Latin word *vulgus*, meaning "crowd." Purity is the sacristan of love, a tribute to mystery, the giving of the primacy to the spiritual over the carnal. Impurity is the using of a person as a means to satisfy one's ego. But purity never allows a material sign to be robbed of its spiritual content. If a youth is pure, he keeps his vital urges controlled until the Divinely appointed time when both God and society sanction their use.

Mozart, the great musician, wrote in this vein to his father, on December 15, 1781: "Nature speaks in me as loudly as in any one else, and I believe with greater force than in the uncultured and the gross. Nevertheless, I refuse to regulate my conduct on the same basis as some young men of my age. On the one side, I have a spirit sincerely religious; I have too much honor and too much love for my neighbor, to deceive any innocent creature. On the other hand, my health is infinitely too precious to hazard it in any passing fancy. I can swear before God, that I can reproach myself with no failure."

Victor Hugo penned the same sentiments to his fiancée in 1820: "It is my desire to be worthy of you, that has made me so severe on myself. If I am constantly preserved from those excesses too common to my age, and which the world so readily excuses, it is not because I have not had a chance to sin; but rather it is that the thought of you constantly preserves me. Thus have I kept intact, thanks to you, the sole treasures I can offer you on the day of marriage; a pure body and a virginal heart."

It is this consciousness of mystery which produces chivalry in the teen-ager, though he does not know its meaning, nor could he explain it. Even the awkwardness of a teen-ager boy before a girl is a sign of awe before a mystery. The timidity of the girl, too, is a sign that there is the guarding of a secret from a too precocious revelation. Whence shame in the young? It is the veil which God has drawn over that mystery until the Divinely appointed time when it may be used as God intended that it should be used. The disgust that follows from the profanation of the mystery is a summons to return to reverence for mystery; it is also a realization that in vain will he snare the music of love who breaks the lute.

The mystery that surrounds the vital impulse is something like the mystery of a flag. The flag of this great country is materially just a piece of cloth. That is what is visible and material about it, but there is something invisible and spiritual about the flag, namely, the tradition and the institutions and the land for which it stands. Americans want to see the flag over their heads, not under anyone's feet. The way we treat our flag is the way youth should treat its energy.

Youth has only one arrow in its quiver; it may be shot but once—that is the arrow of youth. Be sure that it hits the target—the Divinely appointed target—love of God, love of country, love of neighbor.

CHAPTER TWELVE

# Fears and Anxieties

A prune has been defined as a worried plum.

A little girl went to her daddy once and said, "Daddy, are you afraid of cows?" "No."

"Are you afraid of snakes?" "No."

"Are you afraid of long woolly worms?" "No."

"Daddy, you aren't afraid of anything but Mama, are you?"

What are worry and fear, which so much concern our modern world? Fear actually is related to love, as are all passions. Fear is the emotion that rises in us when there is a danger facing something or someone that we love, *e.g.*, our good name, our children, our fortune. The catalogue of fears is the catalogue of loves. Love is attraction for an object; fear is flight from it. Fear is a flight from a future evil which so exceeds our power that we cannot bear up under it. Some of the effects of fear on the ego are the following:

1. Laziness.
2. Gambling.
3. Hypochondria.

4. Lying.
5. Shamefacedness.

One of the first effects of fear is laziness. A person so loves his own physical comfort that he is afraid of work.

I heard of an old couple down South; the husband was leaning against the house, facing the road, and the wife was in the rocker, but she was facing the house. She said, "What's that noise out in front?"

He said, "That's Jim McComb's funeral going by. Big one; about twenty hacks."

"My," she said, "I would love to see that funeral. I wish I was turned around the other way."

Another effect of fear is gambling. A professional gambler is one who is unconsciously afraid of the responsibilities of life and particularly poverty; so he lives in a world of fantasy and dreams in which he is always just about to become rich. He sees himself making a vast fortune and thus gaining domination over his life and environment.

Another effect of fear is hypochondria. There are some people who make themselves mentally sick. Actually, there are cases on record, for example, of men saying, "If I had not been sick, I would have been one of the greatest tennis players in America," "If I had not been sick, I would have written one of the finest novels that has ever been produced," "If I had not been sick, I would have been a millionaire," etc. Such people induce sickness out of fear of being called upon to fulfill their boasts or out of fear of their weakness and ignorance being discovered.

Lying also is a result of fear. If someone has a feeling of deep inferiority, he discovers that by boastfulness and exaggeration he can convince others of the importance of his worth. A little girl was always lying. She was given a St. Bernard dog. I once had a St. Bernard dog; he had the instincts of a lap dog and the instep of a rhinoceros. This little girl went out and told all the neighbors that she had been given a lion. The mother called her and said, "I told you not to lie. You go upstairs and tell God you are sorry. Promise God you will not lie again."

She went upstairs and said her prayers and then came down. Her mother said, "Did you tell God you are sorry?"

The little girl said, "Yes, I did. And God said that sometimes he finds it hard to tell a dog from a lion."

Shamefacedness, or red-facedness, during embarrassing moments is due to fear. The danger of being discovered and losing one's reputation sometimes makes people boorish and loud. Every bully is a coward; his "toughness" and apparent indifference to others' feelings are at bottom a fear of his own insignificance being revealed. "Was my face red" is an expression that covers those moments when caught in acts which embarrass the ego. The story of the woman caught in adultery is a typical case of shamefacedness.

A man was seated next to a very charming lady at a banquet table. He had never met her before, and for want of something better to say he referred to someone he saw at the far end of the room whom he knew, saying, "See that man down there?"

"Yes," said the lady.

"I hate him."

And she, in righteous indignation, said, "I beg your pardon! That is my husband!"

And he said, "Madam, that is why I hate him."

Not everybody gets out of difficulties quite so easily.

The difference between normal fears and anxieties is this:

Normal fears are physical. Abnormal fears or anxieties are psychical or mental.

Normal fears derive from an *object* external to us, such as an explosion or a tiger. Abnormal fears or anxieties come from the *subject*, that is, our inner self.

It is normal to fear what may happen on the outside. The abnormal anxiety—and this is a very modern one—is fear because of something that happens inside of us.

Many minds today look like this on the inside:

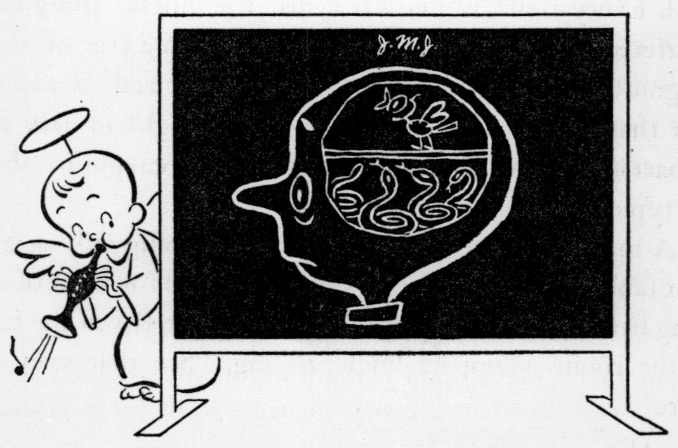

The upper half is the conscious mind, which meets people, keeps up a "good front," and apparently is happy. The lower half is a snake pit—full of coiled serpents always about to emerge into the conscious mind.

Lady Macbeth encourages her husband to murder the King, Duncan, while he sleeps, in order that he may seize the crown and become king. After the murder, Lady Macbeth says to him, "These deeds must not be thought."

In other words, do not think of your guilt, suppress it. Lady Macbeth then kills the grooms, smears them with their own blood, and says to Macbeth, "My hands are of your color, but I shame to wear a heart so white. . . . A little water will clear us of the deed."

The assumption of Lady Macbeth was that there is no such thing as guilt; one merely has to clear oneself of the external consequences. If she lived today, she would say all she had to do was to be psychoanalyzed to get rid of that "false feeling of guilt."

But conscience is not so easily silenced. While Lady Macbeth sleeps, her conscience is awake. She walks in her sleep; she sees blood on her hands, or at least she thinks she does, and says:

> What! Will these hands ne'er be clean? . . .
> Here's the smell of the blood still:
> All the perfumes of Arabia
> Will not sweeten this little hand. . . .

She finally develops a compulsion neurosis which prompts her to wash her hands every quarter of an hour. Instead of purifying her conscience, the compulsion neurosis comes out in the purifying of her hands. Many of the compulsion neuroses in our modern world are due to the same cause: a fear of punishment due to some deep, unabsolved sense of guilt. People dread what they deserve, but having denied their sin, they punish themselves instead of seeking the mercy of God. The language of religion talks of the "Justice of God" when He is neglected; the language of psychology can only say that the God-image, when ignored or repressed, acts on the health and disturbs the mind.

The second effect of this long subjective fear and anxiety is terror. Terror is fear in those who practice terror; it is a dread that seizes a person who is cruel to others. I once asked one of the great artists of our day what he considered the most interesting face in America. He mentioned the name of the then representative of the Soviet Union to the United Nations. He said, "His face intrigues me. If I were painting it, I should paint a skull. He is full of the fear of death."

It is a well-known fact that some representatives of the Soviets, when they checked out of certain hotels in New York, sometimes forgot their guns under the pillows or the bullets in the night tables. They had so much terrorized other people that they constantly lived in terror, even of their own fellow Communists. This terror is a form of fear and cowardice. History proves that such individuals, when they face death, are the most cowardly of men; witness the death of some terrorists of the French Revolution.

Finally, there is horror, or dread. Dread is the fear of nothingness. Think of how many there are in our world today with no plan of life. Animals do not have such subjective fear, because an animal does not have an eternal destiny. Pigs do not worry. But man lives between two worlds. On the one hand, he has a yearning for the infinite, which he cannot escape. On the other hand, he often settles for the finite and thus runs up against the wall of nonexistence. He may be likened to a sailor on a rope ladder during a storm at sea.

Modern man is uncertain of his destiny. He is *always* afraid of being thrown back into the nothingness from which he came, and he doubts whether there is anything at the top of the ladder. The result is dread. Much of modern culture is directed to the suppression of that dread: sleeping tablets, opiates, constant search for pleasures—all these are attempts to suppress this awful, gnawing dread of nothingness. Why is it that a cow never has dread? The reason is that no animal has a soul capable of knowing the infinite. If man were like an ant, a creature only of this world, he would never despair; it takes eternity to make a man despair.

If we only knew it, we are fearing the wrong things. We used to fear God; now we fear our fellow man. The negative side of fear is dread, but the positive side is longing. Once such an individual turns to God, his fear turns to yearning and he discovers peace.

The right kind of fear can be the pathway to peace. There are two kinds of fear, the servile fear and the filial fear.

Servile fear is the fear of punishment, such as citizens have for a cruel dictator. Filial fear is the fear of hurting someone we love. A child disobeys his mother; he may do one of two things. He may say, "Mommy, I am sorry I did wrong. Now I can't go to the movies, can I?" That is servile fear. He might also throw his arms around the mother's neck and say, "Mommy, I am sorry I hurt you." That is filial fear.

Servile fear, or the fear of punishment, or dread, can be the starting point for filial fear. Dread can become longing. Without God, souls have misery but not mercy; they have the wounds, but not the Physician. Misery is anxiety without God; Mercy is anxiety with God.

When there is only servile fear, God seems to be Wrath. To every criminal a judge seems severe. Once, however, we turn from sin, He Who seemed to be Wrath is actually Mercy.

God seems Wrath only to those who refuse to make use of His Forgiveness.

When we say we fear God, we mean we shrink from hurting One Whom we love. But to love that way is to banish all servile fear. That is what the Scriptures mean in saying, "Perfect love casteth out fear."

## CHAPTER THIRTEEN

# Communism and Russia

Russia is constantly in the news! To keep ourselves informed, a word about:

1. The history of Russia.
2. The psychology of the Russian people.
3. What the *Voice of America* might do to help Russia and the world.

In the year 988, Russia began to be Christian. It had only a little more than two centuries in which to develop that faith unmolested, for in the year 1224 the Tartar invasion began. This set up between the Western world and Russia the first Iron Curtain. The year 1224 was that in which the greatest mind that ever lived was born, Thomas Aquinas. When, in the Western world, Aquinas and Bonaventure were teaching, and Francis and Dominic were preaching, when stones could no longer be silent and burst into Gothic cathedrals, when the many great medieval cultures began to flower and bloom, this Iron Curtain was pulled down by the conquerors, and Russia was shut off from all cultural influences of the Western world.

Not until the end of the seventeenth century did Russia open its windows again on the Western world. But by this time it looked upon a world that had lost its Christian unity. Agnosticism, doubt, atheism, rationalism were general in Europe. Peter the Great, beginning in 1697, spent eighteen months

traveling through Europe. Eight of those months he spent learning the trade of shipbuilding. The Russian peasants said of him on his return, "Peter the Great left, but Antichrist came back." When the Grandees came to congratulate him on his return, he personally put them all in chains. He brought back into Russia not the best of the ideas of the Western world. Impressed by the European idea of certain established churches, he introduced secularism in religion through the Synod, which put the Russian Church under the domination of the state. God now became subservient to Caesar.

He killed his own son, who loved the Russian tradition; split Russia into two groups—the masses and the intellectuals. The masses surrendered to his ideas under persecution, while the intellectuals became antireligious. The undercurrent of nihilism, anarchism, and atheism produced in the Western world a static culture of secularism which has endured to this day. But in Russia, these demonic and violent forces prepared a dynamic revolution against all standards.

The next contact of great importance between Russia and Europe took place over two hundred years later, when Germany gave to the world the philosophy of Communism. Many think that Communism is Russian in origin. The fact is that the philosophy of Communism is German in origin, inasmuch as it was conceived in the brain of a German, Karl Marx. He took his philosophy from Germany, his sociology from France, and his economics from England. The philosophy of Communism that spread into Russia was a hodgepodge and a potpourri of the dialectics of Hegel and the materialism of Feuerbach.

What interests us now is how Communism got started in Russia. The philosophy of Communism was already in Russia long before this incident we are about to describe. There was also an already fertile soil in the undercurrent of nihilism introduced by Peter the Great. Lenin was the one who started the Revolution in Russia, and Lenin was Russian. When Lenin went into hiding after the July uprising of 1917, he took two books with him: Marx's *Civil War* and Klausewitz's *On War*. The first taught Lenin what to do with power; the second, how to conquer power. Lenin combined both ideas in his statement that war is not a political act but the instrument of politics. During World War I, the German Ambassador to Moscow, Count Brockdorff Rantzau, suggested that Russia be wooed from the Allies by starting a revolution in Russia. Generals Kaufmann and Ludendorff, of the German General Staff, in March, 1917, locked thirty-two revolutionists in a boxcar and sent them into Russia to start the Revolution. Lenin was in that boxcar. In a short time, the Revolution was on.

A word now about the Russian people. When talking about the psychology of the people, one should always pick out the good traits. There is something bad in all people; but there is also something good. There is even something bad in the Irish! This is about the only nationality I can safely talk about on television and get away with it.

The first characteristic note of the Russian people is universalism or brotherhood. The Russians feel themselves brothers of all men; they love mankind in a mass. Their word *sobor* signifies the idea of fellowship, solidarity, and union with mankind, which Dostoievski in his speech at Pushkin's anniversary on June 6, 1880, summarized: "The Russian heart is most inclined to an all-human, brotherly affection." Many Russian writers feel Russia has been called upon to be a bond of the East and West, situated as it is between Asia and Europe. Soloviev ridiculed the modern Western idea of denying the soul of a man and reducing him to a beast. His argument against such degeneration of human character was that it destroyed the possibility of union between peoples. In order to show the impossibility of any kind of affection between men who were beasts, he satirized the idea with the words "We are descended from apes; therefore, let us love one another."

Unfortunately, this spiritual concept of brotherhood has been secularized. Alexander I in 1814 cherished the idea suggested by Abbé Piatolli that all Europe would be under Russian domination. Some historians have held that the Napoleonic invasion of Russia was an attempt to stop a world domination which was the result of a perverted brotherhood. Napoleon said, "When Russia gets its foot on the Dardanelles, the old world will be enslaved and liberty will have fled to the United States. . . . Europe will be divided like the cities of God before the Kings of Macedonia, and it will have the same sad destiny."

No one, however, has spoiled and prostituted this fine spirit of brotherhood as have the Communists, who have turned universalism into imperialism, and the deep sense of world unity by love, into world tyrannization by hate. The Communist error is to believe that if all people share the same property, they will therefore be brothers. This is a grave fallacy; sharing the same apple does not make men brothers, but if men are brothers, they will share the same apple. Communistic imperialism has been carried out on such a vast scale that today thirty-seven out of every one hundred people in the world have been victimized by the hammer and the sickle.

The second characteristic note of the Russian people is a diffused sense of guilt. There is a right and proper sense in which the human race may feel guilty, and that is in the sense of St. Paul, who writes, "we have all sinned" and stand in need of redemption. At the Last Supper, each one present said, "Lord, is it I?" for in the face of Innocence, no one can be sure that he is innocent. But the Russian sense of guilt is quite different. The Russian people readily feel themselves guilty, even though they have not committed a crime. Here in America it is difficult to convince an individual that he has ever done wrong, but a Russian will confess himself to be guilty of almost anything. As far back as 1892, a writer in Russia described with mathematical certitude that a person arrested on suspicion with no legal proof of guilt will take the judge into confidence and will make a confession of guilt. Of sixty-five criminal cases, seventeen of whom were caught red-handed, leaving only forty-eight under suspicion, all forty-eight were convicted on their own confession.

As a result of their universalism, they feel that in some way the guilt of the world is upon them. They are willing to absorb the guilt of others as their own. This can be a very true religious sentiment, as a man will pay another's debt or share in another's shame or take a blow on the cheek without returning it. The Russians carry this to extreme in their notion of the *Yurodivy*, or the "foreign fool," who takes upon himself in prison camp the punishment that the Communists give out, in order that the evil of the world may thereby be diminished.

As the Communists perverted the notion of brotherhood into world imperialism, so, too, they have perverted the sense of diffused guilt by denying God, denying morality, denying conscience, but keeping confession and guilt. The only guilt that any person can be guilty of in their theology is to sin against the revolutionary philosophy. Their confession is not the free confession of the Western Christian world, but confession in which the soul itself is tortured to confess something that it never committed. To facilitate this, they destroy the spirit by drugs, the mind by torture. After Cardinal Mindzenty was made to stand before a blazing light for seventy-two hours, a psychiatrist who had studied the Soviet methods of psychiatric cruelty boasted that he could keep the outward appearance of the Cardinal normal and, nevertheless, make him avow to any crime the Communists desired. Actually failing in this, the psychiatrist in anger said, "Why is it that Jesus could drive the devil out of a man, but we cannot put the devil into a man?" When an American citizen, Mr. Vogeler, was arrested in Budapest, the Communist prosecuting attorney said, "If God Almighty were there in that chair, we could make Him confess to anything we wanted Him to confess." Thus, the free moral confession of the soul is now turned into a forced, political, irrational disclosure which is the very destruction of personality.

A final word about the *Voice of America* and our propaganda to Russia. Suppose we try to place ourselves within the Russian mentality. I wonder what they think when they hear us boast of our economic superiority? There are many in America who say that all we need to do to incite a revolution in Russia is to drop Sears-Roebuck catalogues on the cities, that the Russian people may know something about our economic standards. They indeed know our technical progress. Gromyko has brought back radio and television sets to Russia—how else could they invent the television set if he did not bring one back?

If we may put ourselves into the Russian mind in the face of this type of propaganda, the Russians might answer us in some such way as this: "All you Americans talk to us about in your broadcasts is your economics and your materialism. It is precisely materialism that has spoiled Russia. You forget that not every people in the world believes in comfort and economic superiority as you do. There are some upon the face of the earth who much prefer an encyclopedia to a deep freeze. You promise us greater economic superiority; so do our Communistic tyrants. You have already sent to us some of your engineers, who have helped forge our chains and tighten our prison bars.

"When people are suffering, they do not want to hear about economics. Our cruel masters have left untouched that which was deepest in our Russian soul, namely *tosha*—our secret ennui—our moral and spiritual longing. We are a people who seem to be eternally uprooted, and if our *dousha*, or soul, does not turn to God, it turns to the devil. In vain, therefore, will you Americans who talk to us about business and security ever fill the void within. If you would win us, speak to us about our soul and the immortal longings of our spirit. It is not from a particular method of economics that we would be liberated, but from the slavery of our spirit.

"Let then the *Voice of America* put on the airways a Jewish rabbi who will protest against the persecution of his own people and who, in the name of God, will promise to us the glorious liberty of the children of God. Let a Protestant minister and a Catholic priest be the oracles on the *Voice of America.* Let them not tell us anything about the materialities of your civilization, but something that the Communists never talk to us about. Speak to us of our *dousha* and our soul. Communism has our body, but it does not have our soul. Use the Name of God. Our Communists are trembling in Russia, lest anyone on the *Voice of America* ever use that Holy Name. They are safe and unafraid of you, so long as you speak to us about your economics and your gadgets and your boasted economic superiority. They can boast of these things, too. We are tired of a Communist revolution because it is not revolutionary enough. It still leaves hate in our souls. You preach to us of the revolution of love—the revolution of the inner freedom of spirit, the revolution that comes from submission to God—and we shall be your brothers under a common Father."

## CHAPTER FOURTEEN

# Character Building

A mother one day said to a school teacher, "I know Reginald has been throwing inkwells out of the window, and throwing spitballs at you, but under no consideration spank Reginald. It will give him a guilt complex. Just hit the boy in front of him, and it will frighten Reginald."

In contrast to that, Lincoln said that a "river always follows the line of least resistance, that is why it is crooked."

Put both these stories together, and you have two views of character training. Books on that subject make it seem so simple and easy. But the practice is much more complicated than the theory.

A human being is very complex, made up of body and soul, flesh and spirit, sensate in his love of pleasure, but rational in his thoughts and ideals. The character each of us creates depends on whether we give the primacy to the body or to the soul. "No man can serve two masters." It is easy to let the body, or the senses, or carnal pleasures dominate. All we have to do is to "let go." But it is very hard to have the spirit and the soul and ideals dominate. This requires a harnessing of the sensate and a disciplining of our lower appetites.

Consider first those who live to satisfy their sensate desires, who never say "No" to what is animal in them, and who identify self-expression with license. They often justify themselves by appealing to evolution, claiming that all progress is automatic and inevitable. This is to forget that there is also operating in nature a law of degeneration which, if we do not resist, pulls us down to what is worse.

Things do not become better by being left alone. A white fence does not get whiter in time. Muscles that are not exercised atrophy. A garden does not evolve into a better garden simply by allowing nature to take its course; the weeds will grow as well as the flowers. If we allow our mind to become fallow and do not pour truth into it by study, not only does ignorance possess it, but we actually reach a point where we can enjoy nothing but picture magazines and cheap novels. The capacity for thought and for discerning truth from error is then surrendered and lost.

Darwin once gave an interesting example of this law of degeneration. He told of a bird fancier who had, with considerable intelligence and effort, developed pigeons into a great variety of markings. He then allowed them to fly into the woods. Years later, he discovered that the black, the white, the striped, the spotted, and the ringed pigeons, which were once distinguishable from one another, had all degenerated into a dark slate blue. Without effort they began to conform to type, which was the lowest common denominator.

Naturalists tell us that the mole once had eyes but chose to grovel in the ground and not use God's sunlight. Nature, as if it were a judge seated in judgment, spoke to the mole and said, "If you will not use the eyes that God has given you, then they shall be taken away." Thus nature spoke the same words of the Saviour, "Take the talent away." St. Paul, in his fine understanding of human nature, warned, "And what excuse shall we have, if we pay no heed. . . ." Nature penalizes the slothful. Organisms that fail to develop themselves deteriorate and become degraded forms of life.

Most educators today forget that there is a bias toward evil in us, and unless this tendency is resisted, character suffers. Biological life is only a temporary endowment and may be well defined as the sum of forces that resist death. When these forces of resistance are neglected, then death ensues.

A man falling from a skyscraper is alive when he passes the fifteenth floor, but the principle of death is in him, though he compliments himself that he is still alive. If a man is poisoned and an antidote is brought to him, it does not make very much difference whether he throws the antidote out of the window or ignores it, as long as he does not take it. The principle of death operates by the mere fact of neglect in the latter case, and in virtue of a kind of law of gravitation in the former, which pulls us down to destruction. Life is a temporary suspension of destructive powers.

We can lose our souls, not only by doing evil, but also by neglecting the good. "I was hungry and you gave Me not to eat." It will generally be found true that those who seek to satisfy their every wish and desire, though they be adults, often suffer from a kind of emotional infantilism; they remain babes all their lives. The characteristic note of a baby is its inability to release itself from emotional instincts; he wants everything and cries until he gets it. He cannot endure the tension between need and satisfaction. Adults in whom the law of degeneration operates have exactly the same tension; they cannot endure, for example, the morning paper not arriving for breakfast, or the coffee being cold, or a wait of five minutes at the barbershop.

I once heard of a man who boarded the Pennsylvania Railroad in Washington, went into the dining car, and ordered anchovies. There were no anchovies. He said to the steward, "I am the Anchovy King of America. I spend $75,000 a year shipping anchovies on the Pennsylvania Railroad; and I come into your dining car and cannot find a single anchovy. Is that good business relationship?"

As soon as the train got to Baltimore, the steward immediately telegraphed ahead to Wilmington, "Rush anchovies!"

They put anchovies on at Wilmington, had them all ready to serve at Philadelphia. The Anchovy King, when he saw them before him, said, "I will not eat them; I would rather be mad."

People who are always wanting their own will are unhappy. The self-centered are the self-disrupted. The man who is self-seeking eventually ends up by hating himself. That is why such a person often tries to "get away from himself," through alcohol, dissipation, and drugs. The self one has to live with can be one's own greatest punishment. To be left forever with that self which we hate is hell. He who starts only loving self ends by hating himself; he becomes like a mansion lying forlorn, spacious, and empty.

The other law which gives primacy to the things of the spirit is what might be called the "law of self-perfection." This involves a certain amount of self-restraint, effort, and discipline to bring the body captive to the mind as the horse is mastered by the driver. As soon as one speaks of self-restraint, one is met by a certain nonthinking group who say, "But you should not repress yourself." If there were ever any nonsense in the world, it is the notion that repression is always wrong. It assumes that nothing should ever be repressed. This is to forget that if you repress evil, good comes up; if you repress good, evil comes up; if you repress the idea that you are going to rob a bank, honesty asserts itself; if a soldier represses the temptation that he ought to sleep while he is on guard, duty asserts itself. The problem is not whether there will be repression or not; it is rather what will be repressed—goodness or evil!

*Amputation* refers to that which is intrinsically evil, *mortification* refers to a mixture of good and evil; *limitation* refers to good. In the physical order, amputation would correspond to an operation for the removal of cancer or a malignant growth. Mortification, which refers to that which is a mixture of good and evil, might be likened to a fever; the fever is not cured by cutting off the head. Limitation would apply to a good thing, such as eating caviar.

*Amputation.* Some evils which afflict human nature cannot be overcome except by a sudden and self-inflicted death. Alcoholism, for example, starts with the free act; the free act becomes a habit; the habit becomes a reflex, and then much of the energy that might have been used by the will to resist

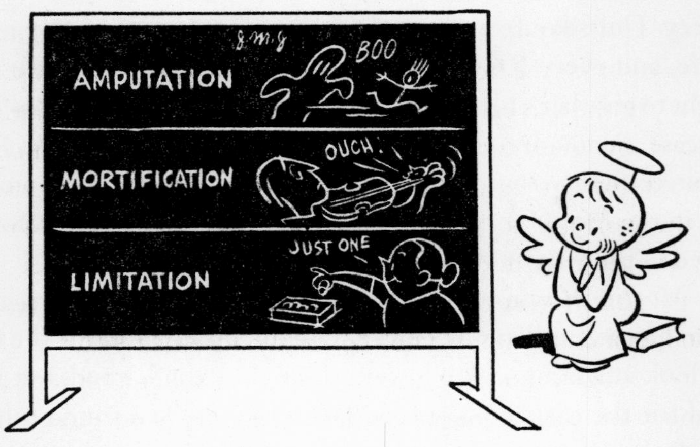


the habit goes into the reflex act. The result is the alcoholic seems to have lost power to resist evil. The question now arises whether it is better with God's grace and with the cooperation of the will to break evil habits off gradually or to amputate them. Our Divine Lord, Who knew human nature better than anyone else, recommended amputation: "If thy right hand is an occasion of falling, cut it off and cast it away from thee." Prolonged gratification is no compensation for gradually diminishing indulgence. If the evil is not eradicated at once, there is both a lingering pain and a diminishing pleasure. Total abstinence is a biological phenomenon as well as a moral recommendation.

Suppose we were talking about wife beating. That is a habit which is intrinsically evil. Certainly it is not to be recommended that it be broken gradually. A husband will not make much sense if he says, "I will break off the habit gradually, but every Thursday from two to three I want the right to beat my wife, and every Friday from seven to seven-thirty I want the right to give her a black eye." Few have many great sins, but one disease is enough to kill a man and bring him to his grave. Precipitate flight from chains that enslave is what a man would do in the face of a tyrant. The same recommendation is counseled in the face of vice.

*Mortification* is to be recommended where there is a mixture of good and evil. The eye is good, but it is bad for the eye to look at a light which is too bright. The ear is good, but it is bad for the ear to subject itself deliberately to a sound which might break the eardrum. Knowing this, one limits the operation of the faculty to what is good and cuts off that which is evil. Applying this to the development of character, as the eye should not look at everything, so neither should the brain look at everything. Though reading is good, one will not put garbage inside the brain. When the wrong kind of ideas get into the mind, they seep down into the unconsciousness and, later on, come out in evil acts.

Hearing is good, but the ear will refuse to listen to Godlessness, backbiting, slander, and evil suggestions. Helping the neighbor is right, but one will also cleanse the good deed of evil motives, for example, giving money in order to be seen and praised by the neighbor. Sociability is good, but one will avoid evil companions; desiring prosperity is good, but desiring to achieve it by cheating the neighbors is evil.

No character ever develops without a certain amount of punishment and resistance and mortification to that which is evil. It will hurt a bit as the violin, if it were conscious, would scream with pain when the violinist tightens the strings. But the violinist would say, "My dear string, this is to give you a better tone." If a block of marble were conscious, it would protest when the chisel strikes, but the sculptor would say, "There is a beautiful form inside of you, and all you have to do is cut away that which is gross, and the inner beauty will be revealed."

*Limitation* refers to that which is good. Wine, caviar, ice cream, lobster, filet mignon are all good. They could become evil only by abusing them, or by taking so much as to destroy our health. A cocktail is good, but ten cocktails taken in succession would be evil. Not long ago I received a letter from someone who said, "I used to take five or six cocktails; now I will take just one. In place of the others I will send the money to you to help your poor people in India." (Hope others follow that good example.) Character is developed by limiting the area of legitimate pleasures. Limiting the good which we enjoy is actually a form of concentration; it is very much like paying more attention to the rose than to the thorn.

It is necessary every now and then to impose hard things

upon ourselves lest we develop faults in a given avocation. I first started teaching in England, which proved that I was very kind to my fellow countrymen and to students. Most teachers begin their profession in their own native country, and the students suffer. But though I tried teaching in another nation before I tried it on my fellow countrymen, I must have been very poor at it. The class that I taught was dogmatic theology in a seminary in London. Some years later, I met one of the students, and he asked if I were still teaching. I told him that I was then teaching philosophy, and he said, "I hope you are a better teacher now than you were then." The point, however, that I wish to bring out is that there were two things I saw very clearly on which I would have to limit myself. The first was to read notes; the second was to sit at my desk while reading the notes. It was very clear that if I ever did either of these two things, I would never be successful as a teacher. It was very hard to get the subject matter so well in my head before class that I could talk on it intelligently to the students; it was less hard, once it was already in my head, to stand instead of sit. But in virtue of limiting two good things, namely, reading and sitting, I made myself a teacher much less insufferable than I would have been otherwise.

Too often, teaching is really nothing else than the communication of information from the notebook of a professor to the notebook of a student, without passing through the mind of either. The reason for standing while talking to the students was in order that information might be communicated with less passivity and with greater energy. As Horace put it, "If you wish people to weep, you must weep first." Truth should always be communicated to students with a certain amount of fire and enthusiasm; but if one is on fire, he cannot sit. No one who is in love with a great cause, and is anxious to pass it on to his fellow man, will sit in pleading that cause. To the credit of Communists, it must be said that they stand when they plead for their tyranny; liberals always sit, and reactionaries always lie flat.

Leaving now the three forms of character building, we come briefly to motives for self-discipline. The reason anyone amputates evil, or mortifies his passion, or limits the good things that he enjoys is because of love. Something has to be repressed in each of us. In order to give carnality a free rein, the aspirations of the spirit have to be suffocated; in order to satisfy the desire of personality for union with Perfect Life and Truth and Love Which is God, instincts and passions which rebel against these ideals must be disciplined and mortified. The best reason for doing it is to reproduce within ourselves the Divine Image and Likeness. The motivation is love.

Love is not only an affirmation; it is also a negation. A man who loves a woman and asks for her hand in marriage by that very fact negates every other woman. A man who affirms the love of God negates the love of evil. A woman who loves a young man will say to him, "Do you like my hair this way? Do you like me in red?" She wants to please him. Those who wish to develop a character of soul act precisely that way before God. The motto of their lives is "All things that are pleasing to Him, that I do." The reason noble characters refuse to sin is not because they are afraid of hell or punishment; they negate evil because they would not hurt the one they love.

As Archbishop Trench wrote more than a century ago:

Could we but crush that ever-craving lust
For bliss, which kills all bliss; and lose our life,
Our barren unit life, to find again
A thousand lives in those for whom we die:
So were we men and women, and should hold
Our rightful place in God's great universe,
Wherein, in heaven and earth, by will and nature,
*Naught* lives for self. All, all, from crown to footstool
The lamb, before the world's foundation slain
The angels, ministers to God's elect;
The sun, who only shines to light a world;
The clouds, whose glory is to die in showers;
The fleeting streams, who in their ocean graves
Flee the decay of stagnant self-content;
The oak, ennobled by the shipwright's axe;
The soil, which yields its marrow to the flower;
The flower, which breeds a thousand velvet worms,
Born only to be prey to every bird—
All spend themselves on others; and shall man,
Whose twofold being is the mystic knot
Which couples earth and heaven—doubly bound,
As being both worm and angel, to that service
By which both worms and angels hold their lives—
Shall he, whose very breath is debt on debt,
Refuse, forsooth, to see what God has made him?
No, let him show himself the creatures' lord

By free-will gift of that self-sacrifice
  Which they, perforce, by nature's law must suffer;
Take up his cross and follow Christ the Lord.

For our next telecast we shall present a comparison of the death of Lenin and the death of Stalin. The death of Lenin will be presented from a historical point of view and the death of Stalin from a literary point of view.

CHAPTER FIFTEEN

# Death of Stalin [1]

There is nothing new in the world. There are only the same old things happening to new people. As Cassius said:

> How many ages hence
> Shall this our lofty scene be acted over,
> In state unborn and accents yet unknown.

In order to prove it, we shall show similarities between three historical events: the death of Lenin, the death of Stalin, and the death of Caesar.

First, *the death of Lenin.* In 1922, the Communists held the Eleventh Party Congress. Molotov was the Secretary of the party, but Stalin induced his friend Antonoviev to move for his nomination. The result was that Molotov was deposed.

In that same year, Lenin suffered two strokes. In 1923, on January 4, Lenin wrote a codicil to his will. The codicil read, "Stalin is crude, rude and insupportable. I propose to remove Stalin and appoint another who is more patient, more loyal, more attentive to comrades and less capricious."

[1] This telecast was given on February 24, 1953. The death of Stalin was announced on March 5, 1953.

At the same time, Lenin's wife said, "Nikolai has just written a letter to Stalin breaking off all relations with him."

In 1924, on the night of January 21, the night that the great Archbishop Ceplak was taken to a more rigorous prison—the last anti-God act of Lenin—a telegraph key was moving up and down slowly in one of the rooms of the Kremlin. Listening to its ticking were Stalin, Zinoviev, Kalinin, Bukharin. The message spelled out, "Lenin is dying." In a sled, speeding over the frozen ground, under the frosty trees, Stalin and his companions came to the deathbed of Lenin. Though doors were barred, guards posted, the sinister figure of Death entered and laid its cold hand on Lenin, who went to meet God.

The will was read. Then there came the question of the funeral and what to do with Trotsky. On January 15 of that very year, Trotsky had left Moscow for Sukhum, the Russian Riviera, in order that he might recuperate from his campaigns. While on his way, Trotsky stopped at the town of Tiflis. Stalin was in a seminary there for a time. Litvinov, it was said, also figured in robbing a bank in Tiflis.

But, at any rate, when Trotsky received the telegram and decoded it, it read, "Lenin is dead."

Trotsky immediately answered, "I must return at all costs to Moscow. When will be the funeral?"

The telegram came back: "The funeral will be held on Saturday. You will not be able to return in time. It is the opinion of the Politburo that you proceed at once to Sukhum on account of your health. (signed) Stalin."

Trotsky, thinking the funeral was to be held on Saturday,

and knowing that he could not be back in time, did not return to Moscow. The funeral was held on Sunday. Trotsky was not there. Stalin preached the funeral oration, and "preached" is the word. He had an atavistic throw-back to his seminary days in Tiflis, and though the sermon was only twenty lines long, five times he addressed Lenin as if he were a god, always speaking to him in the scriptural second person singular. Five times Stalin said, "Thou art our leader, Lenin, and we will obey Thy command," as Mark Antony in his funeral oration five times said, "And Brutus is an honorable man."

Now begins the struggle for power. There was established in Russia at this time a troika, or triumvirate. The triumvirate consisted of Stalin, Kamenev, and Zinoviev. Zinoviev was the head of the Communists in Leningrad and also the president of the Soviet International. Kamenev was the head of the Soviet in Moscow. In May, 1924, Stalin offered to resign at the Thirteenth Congress because of the will of Lenin, who was against his succession, but his offer was refused.

The first step Stalin took to assure himself of power was to get rid of Trotsky. Stalin wrote a pamphlet entitled "Trotskyism and Lenin"; Kamenev wrote on "Lenin and Trotskyism" and Zinoviev on "Bolshevism and Trotskyism." The point at issue was whether the revolution should be attempted all over the world at once or in one country first. Trotsky was supposed to have favored world revolution immediately.

The second step was to induce Trotsky to publish the *Letters of October*. The *Letters* revealed that Kamenev and Zinoviev were Mensheviks and not Bolsheviks. Mensheviks believed in parliamentary reform, and Bolsheviks believed in revolution. Lenin described the difference: An apple is on the tree. A Menshevik waits for it to fall; the Bolsheviks knock it down.

When Stalin heard that the companions who nominated him were Mensheviks, he pretended to be scandalized. He hired a prosecutor, who sentenced them to death. The Soviet prosecutor was no other than Andrei Vishinsky. In 1936, they were lined up against a wall of the Kremlin and shot. At the time, the widow of Lenin said, "If Lenin were living today, he would be in prison."

Trotsky was exiled by Stalin to Siberia, then finally made his way to Mexico, where one of the agents of the Soviet found him and ran an ice pick into his neck. Thus Stalin ended his triumvirate and began his mastery in Russia.

There is nothing new in the murder, scheming, and intrigue of this triumvirate. There was another like it in Rome, on the occasion of the death of Julius Caesar. After his assassination, three men vied for his power: Cassius, Mark Antony, and Brutus.

Just before the assassination, Julius Caesar compared himself to a god, as Stalin had compared Lenin to God, and later on allowed himself to be deified. This is the speech of Julius Caesar as given by Shakespeare:

*Stalin:*

But I am constant as the Northern Star,
  Of whose true-fix'd and resting quality
There is no fellow in the firmament.

The skies are painted with unnumber'd sparks,
They are all fire, and every one doth shine;
But, there's but one in all doth hold his place:
So, in the world; 'tis furnish'd well with men,
And men are flesh and blood, and apprehensive;
Yet in the number, I do know but one
That unassailable holds on his rank,
Unshak'd of motion: and that I am he . . .

Caesar made himself a god and then perished. Stalin made himself a god, and he too will perish. In 1937, on December 21, Moscow ordered published a poem concerning his divinity; this poem was telegraphed to the United States and was published in the Communist sheet of New York, *The Daily Worker*, on December 31, 1937.[1]

Above the valley
The mountain peak;
Above the peak
The sky;
But Stalin,
Skies have no height
To equal you,—
Only your thoughts
Rise higher.
The stars, the moon
Pale before the sun
That pales in turn
Before your shining mind.

Suppose we go back to Shakespeare and show there is nothing new in the world. We are not concerned about the manner

[1] Composed by a Soviet woman and sent to the United States; translated by Isidore Schneider.

of Stalin's death. But Stalin must one day meet his judgment. We are concerned with another troika, another triumvirate after Caesar's death.

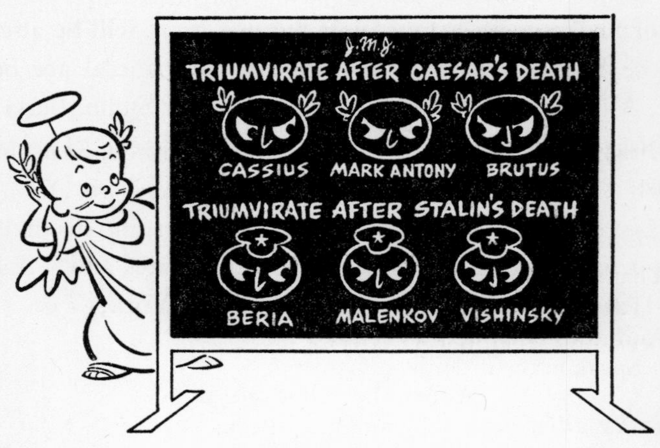


Cassius was a crude character and prefigures Beria, who is the head of the secret police of Russia, the villain behind the knock-at-the-door-at-night terrorism. He is also the head of the atomic-bomb manufacture in Russia and the whip over all labor camps.

Mark Antony, appearing friendly with Caesar, is very much like Malenkov. Malenkov at one time was private secretary to Stalin, long in his counsel, recently appointed to the Presidium, the one most likely to succeed him.

Brutus, the most learned of the group, who knew other civilizations, corresponds to someone who is rather familiar with Western civilization; his name is Vishinsky.

Now, let us read Shakespeare's *Julius Caesar*. We shall not change any lines of Shakespeare, but only a few words. For Caesar, we shall read "Stalin," for Rome we shall read "Moscow," and for Roman we shall read "Soviet." Remember, no lines of Shakespeare's tragedy of *Julius Caesar* will be altered. Suppose Stalin is dead. The plans for the funeral are being made. All three want to talk at the funeral of Stalin. Beria and Vishinsky are afraid to allow Malenkov to speak. The latter pleads:

*Malenkov:*

That's all I seek: . . . that I may
  Produce his body to the market-place;
And in the pulpit, as becomes a friend,
  Speak in the order of his funeral.

*Vishinsky answers:*

You shall, Malenkov.

Now Beria speaks. As a policeman, he keeps rather quiet. But he is angry at Vishinsky for allowing Malenkov to speak:

*Beria:*

Vishinsky, a word with you.
(Aside to Vishinsky)
  You know not what you do; do not consent
That Malenkov speak in his funeral:
  Know you how much the people may be mov'd
By that which he will utter?

*Vishinsky:* (answers Beria)

I'll talk!—And say Malenkov talks by permission.
  By your pardon;

I will myself into the pulpit first
  And show the reason for our Stalin's death:
What Malenkov shall speak, I will protest
  He speaks by leave and by permission . . .

*Beria:* (still not wanting Malenkov to speak)

I know not what may fall; I like it not.

*Vishinsky:* (reprimands Malenkov in arrogant fashion and tells him what to say)

Malenkov, here, take you Stalin's body.
  You shall not in your funeral speech blame us,
But speak all good you can devise of Stalin,
  And say you do 't by our permission;
Else shall you not have any hand at all
  About his funeral: and you shall speak
In the same pulpit whereto I am going,
  After my speech is ended.

*Malenkov:*

Be it so;
  I do desire no more.

*Vishinsky:* (to Beria)

Go you into the other street,
  And part the numbers.

So Beria goes to the side streets to take care of the crowds. Vishinsky gives the funeral oration over Stalin, using the familiar slogans we heard him shriek at the UN. How true the words of Shakespeare ring!

*Vishinsky:*

Stoop, Soviets, stoop
  And let us bathe our hands in Stalin's blood

Up to the elbows, and besmear our swords
  Then walk we forth, even to the marketplace,
And waving our red weapons o'er our heads
  Let's all cry 'Peace, Freedom and Liberty!'

And now *Malenkov* speaks:

Friends, Soviets, countrymen, lend me your ears;
  I come to *bury* Stalin, not to *praise* him.
The evil that men do lives after them,
  The good is oft interred with their bones;
*So* let it be with Stalin. The *noble* Vishinsky
  Hath told you Stalin was ambitious;
If it were so, it was a grievous fault,
  And grievously hath Stalin answer'd it.
Here, under leave of Vishinsky, and the rest—
  For Vishinsky is an honourable man;
So are they all, all honourable men—
  Come I to speak in Stalin's funeral.
He was my friend, faithful and just to me
  But Vishinsky says he was ambitious;
And Vishinsky is an honourable man. . . .

  But yesterday, the word of Stalin might
Have stood against the world: Now he lies there
  And none so poor to do him reverence.

. . . Now do I prophesy . . .
  A curse shall light upon the limbs of men;
Domestic fury and fierce civil strife
  Shall cumber all the parts of Russia:
Blood and destruction shall be so in use,
  And dreadful objects so familiar,
That mothers shall but smile when they behold
  Their infants quarter'd with the hands of war.
All pity chok'd with custom of fell deeds:
  And Stalin's spirit, ranging for revenge,

With Hate by his side come hot from hell,
  Shall in these confines with a dictator's voice
Cry "Havoc!"

Thus ends the funeral oration over Caesar, and the funeral oration over Stalin. The death of Stalin will also be the end of the troika, or triumvirate. Even if this speech of Shakespeare, which we put into the mouth of Malenkov, should ever come true, it will not be the beginning of peace in the world. Stalin's evil spirit is ranging through the world crying "Havoc" or revolution. Peace will come only with another spirit, which is the spirit of the love of God and the love of man that seizes the hearts of men. May God come to us and to the godless in Russia.

## CHAPTER SIXTEEN

# Tolerance

Have you noticed how many blackboards now are appearing on television programs? But none of them have angels. Many inducements have been held out to our angel. He has been offered angel cake for a year by a flour company, while a rival network offered him a year's supply of Halo shampoo. An aviation company promised to supply him, not only with new wings, if he needed them, but also a new fuselage. But our angel has decided to stay with us; he feels that he could render much greater benefaction to mankind by erasing as quickly as possible my horrible drawings.

I must tell you the story about our angel. Heaven sent him on a recent commission, not very long ago, to two Irishmen who were fighting. These two Irishmen, Murphy and Kelly, were bitter rivals. An angel was sent down to pacify Murphy. "Listen, Murphy, you are very bitter and cold and cruel toward Kelly; to cure you, the Good Lord has promised to give you one of anything in the world, if you will only let Kelly have two of them."

"Well," Murphy said, "if I am the head of one labor union down on the docks, does that mean Kelly will be the head of two labor unions?"

"Yes," said the angel.

"Does that mean if I win the Irish Sweepstakes once, Kelly wins them twice?"

The angel said, "That's right."

"And it means that if I have a brass band following me, that Kelly has one following him and also one playing before him?"

"Yes."

Murphy said, "Angel, I'll take a glass eye."

I am glad my angel told me that story; it is a very fitting start for the telecast, which is on tolerance.

Tolerance is related to patience, justice, equality, and charity. The definition we shall give is in Latin. The Latin words are similar to English words; so you can readily translate:

*Toleratio est permissio negativa mali.*

Literally, it means that tolerance is a negative permission of evil, a patient forbearance in the face of evil, either real evil or imaginary. Notice that tolerance is *negative*. Tolerance is never positive. If it were, it would be connivance with evil. No man should be tolerant during a holdup. At least he could call the police.

There are certain principles concerning tolerance that need to be understood:

1. Tolerance never refers to persons.

2. Tolerance always refers to evil, real or imaginary, never to good.

Let us take this second one first: tolerance never refers to good. The good is never to be tolerated; rather it is to be approved; aye! it is to be loved. You never say, "I'll tolerate a beefsteak dinner." Do you tolerate patriotism? Do you tolerate science? During the past few weeks, some good souls sent the equivalent of a couple of bottles of whisky which they decided to forgo for the sake of our poor foreign missions. I certainly do not tolerate such acts of charity. I approve them and wish more would do likewise.

Can you imagine a love song in which one changes the word "love" to tolerate? "I tolerate you in June, under the moon." How absurd it is! Tolerance never refers to the good. No woman tolerates a mink coat.

It refers to evil, a physical evil, a moral evil, an intellectual evil; but it is evil, real or imaginary. Sometimes the opinions of others that we regard as evil actually are not evil at all but are very good. Sometimes your opinions may seem good to you, but objectively they may be evil. So evil may be either real or imaginary, but tolerance always refers to evil and never to good.

One of the things to which tolerance may be applied is "pet peeves" such as reading a newspaper in the wife's face at breakfast, snoring in Pullmans, smoking pipes in the parlor, or drinking soup noisily. I heard of an Englishman once who, whenever he ate alphabet soup, dropped all of his H's.

Tolerance must be practiced by husbands whose wives are backseat drivers. Ed Wynn tells a beautiful story about a backseat driver. He said, "The husband and wife were one day out automobile riding, and the automobile stopped in the middle of a railroad track.

"The wife shouted, 'Here comes a train; hurry up and get the car over.'

"The husband said, 'I've got my end over; you get yours.' "

We also have to tolerate the opinions of others. We may not agree with them; we may think they are very wrong; we may even think their opinion is evil. But, granted that it is, great patience and forbearance should be practiced because they are entitled to assert their own particular point of view.

*Tolerance never refers to persons.*

If there is anything that makes me feel sad at heart, it is to see a cartoon or a drawing or a picture, for example, of a Chinese child, a Japanese child, an American child, and underneath it the caption reads, "Be tolerant." A person is the most precious thing in the universe. A person is made in the image and likeness of God: every person bears within himself the Divine resemblance. The state exists for the person, and not the person for the state. No Irishman is to be tolerated! No Jew is to be tolerated! No American is to be tolerated! No German is to be tolerated! As persons, they are all *to be loved*. We have misunderstood tolerance when we say that one must be tolerant to certain persons.

We may be tolerant of their acts, we may be tolerant of their deeds, we may be tolerant of their thoughts, but, as persons, they are endowed with sovereign, inalienable worth. The whole universe exists for them. The Saviour died for them; if we are merely tolerant to them, we offend both their dignity and our own.

Are there any limits to tolerance? Many would deny it, saying we should be tolerant under all circumstances, because intolerance is always wrong. This is not true. Tolerance is not always right, and intolerance is not always wrong.

The limit of tolerance is reached when tolerance would deprive someone of sovereign inalienable rights. Suppose you are sick; suppose you have pneumonia. The doctor examines you and says, "You are very sick; your body is full of pneumococci germs and streptococci germs and some other cocci germs. But we must be broad-minded about these evils. I find your body is a particularly fertile field for developing these germs. Instead of curing you, I am going to make a study of pneumonia as it exists in you." Are you tolerant? You say, "No! Tolerance never goes that far." In other words, you are very intolerant about your life.

*Liberty:* Is there a limit to tolerance, say, of freedom of speech? Yes, there is a limit to freedom of speech. It is reached when we use freedom of speech to destroy freedom of speech. Anyone in the world may use freedom of speech, as long as he allows anyone else to enjoy that freedom of speech. But there are those who would use this freedom of speech to deny that right to others. Toward that latter group we ought to be intolerant. That is why the Communists differ from any other group in a democracy. Even those people who are called "crackpots" are willing to let anyone else be a "crackpot." But Communists will not allow anyone to be a non-Communist.

They would set up a regime such as they have in Russia, which would deny freedom of press, freedom of speech, freedom of conscience. To such enemies of freedom there must be a reminder that they may enjoy freedom of speech on condition that if they were in power, they would extend it to others. As Chief Justice Holmes said, "Freedom of speech does not mean the right to shout 'fire!' in a theater."

Should we be tolerant of persecution of the Chinese, five million of whom have already been liquidated by the Communists? Should we be tolerant and falsely "broad-minded" of the persecution of the Jews and others in Russia? All these people are persons and have the sovereign worth of which we have spoken. The democratic world must rise up in defense of the right kind of tolerance and say, "These people are entitled to the pursuit of happiness, free speech, and to a government of their own choosing, and as God-fearing people we will help them preserve these rights."

Tolerance refers to evil. Love refers to persons. A teacher is intolerant about Washington being the capital of the United States, and not Moscow, but the pupil is not beaten for her error. If you go into a grocery store and the grocer adds $24 and $7 and makes it $43, you are very intolerant about the truth, which is $31; but you do not cut off the grocer's head. If he said, "But Einstein said everything is relative," you would answer, "Not so relative that we have four toes on one foot counted one way and six toes on the other foot counted the other way." Life is intolerant of death. Truth is intolerant of error; Love is intolerant of hate. But the sick, the erring, and the Communists are to be loved.

We must love persons. You may love persons in one of four ways. You may love them with the *utilitarian* love; you may love them with a *romantic* love; you may love with a *democratic* love; or you may love with a *Divine* love.

To love someone with a utilitarian love is to love him because he is useful to you. "He can get it for you wholesale," or as I overheard someone say the other day, "You've been in New York three weeks and still buy retail?" Utilitarian love is not a very high kind of love: "Sure, let's visit the Joneses, they always serve the best Scotch."

Romantic love is the love we have for someone simply because of the pleasure that particular person gives. This is often the basis of modern marriages, in which a person does not love another person, but the pleasure which the other person occasions. Such people are not in love with persons; they are in love with an experience. When the experience grows stale, then love disappears.

Democratic love is based on the equality of all persons. Our democracy is based on the idea that everyone, independent of his religion or color or race, is entitled to all the advantages of our government and equal rights under the Constitution.

We love persons divinely when we recognize the Divine Image in their souls, that they are made in the image and likeness of God and are either real or potential children of God through grace. Our Blessed Lord gave the commandment

"Thou shalt love the Lord thy God with the love of thy whole heart, and thy whole soul, and thy whole mind, and thy whole strength." This is the first commandment, and the second, its like, is this: "Thou shalt love thy neighbour as thyself." The present tendency is to isolate the second commandment from the first; to speak of a "brotherhood of man" without the "Fatherhood of God." It is a terrible thing for a man not to know his own father. Will they make humanity a brood of illegitimate children?

Take the second commandment, "Thou shalt love thy neighbour as thyself." Notice that Our Blessed Lord said, "*Love* thy neighbor." He does not say, "*Like* your neighbor"; He does not say, "*Tolerate* your neighbor." He also called it a *commandment*. "A new commandment I give." There is a world of difference between *loving* and *liking*. Liking is in the *emotion;* loving is in the *will*. Liking is not subject completely to our control, but love can be commanded. Liking is a kind of reaction like a hiccough; loving is a decision or a resolution. We cannot *like* everyone, but we can *love* everyone.

There are certain things that we cannot help not liking. Some people do not like olives. I do not like chicken. Every five years I announce that over the radio and television, so that when I am invited out, I will not get chicken for dinner. Time is pressing too quickly to tell you why, except that it has to do with being served too much chicken on a farm during summer vacation as a boy. I had to wring a chicken's neck every noon.

You may not *like* medicine, but your will *commands* you to take it for the good of your health. You may not *like* somebody, but you can still *love* him, because loving is a duty; it is good for your soul, and it also glorifies God. If you do an injury to someone you do not *like*, you will dislike him still more; if you do a favor to someone you do not like, you will love him more.

"Love thy neighbor." The neighbor is the person next door. The neighbor is my other-self. The neighbor is a person you meet. The neighbor is the touchstone and test for determining whether I am selfish. Our Blessed Lord did not say, "Love your *friends;* love those who love you," for there is no reward in that. But "Love your neighbor."

When you women are out shopping, the neighbor is the lady who pulls the dress out of your hand when you want to buy it.

When you and someone else run to get a seat on the bus, the other person is the neighbor. When you are driving in Sunday traffic, the one who cuts left from the far lane is your neighbor. The neighbor is the one who steps on your toes in the subway; the neighbor is the one who comes to a meeting or conference with you, is very nice to your face, but when the meeting is over, runs a knife into your back.

Our Lord never said, "Love humanity." It is too vague and allows the individual to escape. Lovers of "humanity" or "the people" often vicariously enjoy the fruits of an idealistic worship, which in the individual instance they make a mockery. It is not unknown that lovers of the brotherhood of man without the Fatherhood of God pay their maids seventeen dollars a week.

The next point is "Love thy neighbor as thyself." How do you love yourself? You certainly love yourself. When you come into the theater, you pick out a pretty good seat for yourself; when you go to buy some clothes, you do not say, "Now this looks very bad on me, but I shall take it anyway." When you look over the bill of fare and some rich relative is paying the bill, you do not order a hamburger.

Though you *love* yourself, still there are some things you do not love about yourself. You do not love yourself when you are "catty"; you do not love yourself when you are unkind to someone; you do not love yourself when someone calls up on the phone, and you, thinking it was someone other than the boss, called him "Old Baldy." You do not love yourself when you are grumpy, insulting, and in general when you make a fool of yourself.

You find you love yourself in prosperity and adversity; when you are hungry and when you are filled; when you are rich and when you are poor; when you are too tired to talk and when you are loquacious. *The neighbor ought to be loved that way.*

Furthermore, what you love about yourself is the image of God in you; what you do not love about yourself is the ruination of that image. We are to love our neighbor that way. We are to love the sinner, but hate the sin. We must always love him as a sinner. We love the Communists, but hate Communism; we love our enemies, but hate their enmity of Justice and Truth. The erring person we receive into the treasury of our souls, but never the error into the treasury of our wisdom.

The inspiration for this kind of love is the Love of One Who came to this earth and gave up His life that we might live. When He was unfurled on the great Cross, He did something that was never done before in the world. As a tree will sometimes bathe with perfume the axe that cuts it, so He let fall from His lips for the first time in the hearing of men the words "Father, forgive them; they know not what they do." "Forgive them"—the neighbors, everybody, you and me.

"Forgive"—Why? "Because they know not what they do."

When someone else does us wrong, we say, "He should have known better." Yet He, with His Divine Wisdom, said, "They do not know what they do." He Who knows all things finds excuses for forgiveness: "This is the greatest love a man can show, that he should lay down his life for his friends; . . ."

The love of God is something like the sun. Those who come very close to God enjoy both the Fire of His Love and the Light of His Truth; those who refuse to come near to the Heat of His Love nevertheless enjoy the Light of His Truth.

CHAPTER SEVENTEEN

# Something Higher

The other day I was in an elevator in a department store. I was shopping on the fifth floor, and I wanted to go to the sixth. I stepped into the elevator and several other passengers entered at the same time.

Just as the elevator was about to start, the operator said, "Going up."

Some woman rushed out madly saying, "I don't want to go up; I want to go down."

Then turning to me—I do not know why she picked on me —she said, "I did not think I could go wrong following you."

I said, "Madam, I only take people *up*, not down."

How to take people "up" is the subject of this telecast.

We begin by summarizing a few philosophies of life through the centuries.

Many have lived for centuries—and many still do—who believe in a moral universe, made up of heaven, earth, and hell.

Heaven
Earth
Hell

Above man (not necessarily in a geographical sense) is Heaven, which must be won; below is hell, which is the den of voluntary failures. During the earthly pilgrimage, man may say "aye" or "nay" to either one of these eternal destinies. *Time*, therefore, is a kind of novitiate for eternity. This philosophy places great responsibilities on human beings.

Within the last two hundred years, the great eternities of heaven and hell have been denied by many.

Man is said to have no other existence than the biological one on the horizontal plane of earth. Given enough pleasure and the opportunity to make enough money, he has all he needs for happiness.

Within the last thirty-five or forty years, this horizontal plane has been shortening. World War I, World War II, depressions have closed man within himself, so that today man is locked up inside of himself. He is almost his own jailer, trapped by his own follies. Just as a river that is blocked collects considerable scum and sediment, so man imprisoned within himself becomes the victim of fears and anxieties.

To give some compensation for the loss of eternal destinies, some psychologists have put three levels inside of the human mind. One level is that of the super ego, which is made up of taboos, ideals, commandments, religion and morality. Down below is the *id*, the deep, mysterious, cavernous instinct to satisfy the animal cravings of man. In the middle is consciousness.

Modern man is imprisoned in the mind, without doors and without windows; about all the enjoyment that he gets out of life is to psychoanalyze the worries that go on inside of him.

Is there any possibility of modern man escaping his inner hell? Modern man is like an egg. An egg can be broken in one of two ways, from the outside or from the inside. It can be broken from the outside by smashing it. Modern society can be broken from the outside. This is the function of barbarism. It may very well be that the purpose of Communism in the modern world is to break the hard shell of materialism that is encrusting modern civilization, in order that the hidden life may spring forth unto a richer and a better culture. That may be under Providence the mission of Communism.

An egg can be broken also from the inside, as a chick picks away and discovers another world. But the chick inside must have the instinct of realizing that there is a bigger and broader world than the mere confines of a shell. Given the greater environment, the chick tries to establish relationship with it by escaping from the shell. It is this latter method we recommend for releasing modern man from the prison house of his own doubts and uncertainties.

How does man establish contact with this new and greater environment and what is its nature? Evolution suggests the answer as we study the various hierarchies of creation:

Man
Animal
Plant
Chemical

If anything lower is ever to mount to a higher plane, two conditions are required:

1. The higher must come down to the lower, or there must be a descent from above.
2. What is lower must surrender its lower existence to what is above it.

Is it possible for the rain and the phosphates and the carbon, moisture and sunlight to enter into the higher life of a plant? To do so, the plant must go down to the chemicals to absorb and assimilate them. If the plant could speak, it would say to the moisture and the sunlight, "Unless you die to your lower existence, you cannot live in my kingdom. You are not blotted out; you are not to be destroyed, for if you were destroyed, you would never live in me and nourish me. Surrender this lower form of existence, and find yourself in me in a living thing."

If plants are ever to live in the animal kingdom, the animals must come down to the plants and consume them. But the second law also must function: the plants must surrender their lower existence. They must be pulled up from their roots, ground beneath the jaws of death. They are not destroyed; otherwise they would never nourish the animals. If the animal could speak, it would say to the plant, "Unless you die yourself, you cannot live in my kingdom." When the plant is taken up into the animal, it is no longer just simply a living thing; it is now part of a creature that is endowed with five senses; it is elevated to a kingdom where there is not only life but sentience, not only existence but self-movement.

When man, in his turn, takes chemicals, plants, and animals into his nature, he practically says to them, "Unless you die yourself, you cannot live in my kingdom." The animal must be subjected to the knife and the fire; the plant must be extracted from its earth environment; the air must submit to containment within lungs. But when these lower things surrender their existence, they are taken up into a higher creature that is a *thinking*, *willing*, and *loving* being; they become part of a richer and higher kingdom, become part of the world of poetry, art and science, culture and civilization.

Why should the law stop with man? Is there not something higher that can come down to man, on the one condition that man die to himself? The rose has no right to say there is no higher life than itself. Man has no right to say there is no higher life than himself. Two little tadpoles were playing in the water. One little tadpole said to the other, "I think I will stick my head above the water and see if there is anything else in this world."

The first tadpole said, "Don't be silly. You mean to say there is something else in this world besides water?" Many human beings are like tadpoles in the sense that they deny there is anything above them into which they can be incorporated.

There is something higher than man in this universe, namely, God. But if man is ever to be elevated to partnership with the Divine, *God must come down to man.* But there is a difference between man going down to lower creation, and God coming to man. These things have no personality, no freedom, no liberties, and no rights; only persons have rights. Animals need never consult the plants; plants need never consult the chemicals. They merely use violence and confiscate without consultation. But no one can ever lay hold of man without exercising or abusing man's freedom. Even God will not do that.

He will not come into the order of humanity without first asking man if he freely will receive Him. God sent an angel to consult a Woman as the representative of humanity. The question was, "Will you freely give me a human nature?" God did come down to earth in the person of Jesus Christ through the free act of a Woman. He willed to lift man to Himself, as man was lifting chemicals, plants, and animals to himself. But He would not constrain man to do so. Assimilation with His Divine Nature would have to be done only through man's free act, just as the Woman's act was free. God forces Himself on no one; He breaks down no doors.

A condition, however, of man uniting himself with God's Nature was that man "die to himself" as the salt "dies" to its nature entering into the life of man. Man would have to die to evil which is in him. Just as the chaff is separated from the wheat, so he must separate evil from himself. Such obstacles as pride, covetousness, lust, anger, envy, gluttony, and sloth—which spoil this ascent of man back again to God—would have to be eliminated. Then as the soul is the life of the body, God would become the life of the soul. His Gospel was "Unless you die to yourselves, you cannot live in My Kingdom."

Not many men want to die to their lower selves; it costs so much. Some prefer to have a cosmic religion, which puts no restraint on their pride, nor curbs their passions.

Apropos of that, some few years ago, on the radio, I was talking about such a cosmic religion, observing, "Man can never love the cosmos because the cosmos is too big and too bulky. No man can ever love anything he cannot get his arm around. That is why God became a man, in order that he might be loved by us."

After the broadcast, I really and truly received a telephone call from a woman who in wrath and exasperation chided me, saying, "Do you mean to tell me that I cannot love anyone unless I can get my arms around him?"

I said, "Madam, that is not my problem; that is yours."

Suppose man does say, "I am willing to die to that which is evil in me in order to be incorporated into Divinity." He is then elevated above human nature, and that order we call supernatural, because it is *super*, over and above, the natural. If I had a bottle here on the desk and that bottle suddenly turned into four roses (do not get me wrong on this), that would be something that does not belong to the nature or power or capacities of a bottle, namely, to bloom.

If a rose suddenly spoke, "I think I will go to California for the winter, or to Florida . . . ," that would be an act that certainly does not belong to the nature or the powers of a rose. If a dog should suddenly walk across our stage here and begin to quote Shakespeare, that would be a very "supernatural" act for a dog.

Now, if man by nature, who is only a creature, becomes a child of God, begins to share the Divine Nature, such a gift does not belong to his nature any more than blooming belongs to a stone or speech belongs to a dog. It would be something so far beyond him that when he received it he would wonder that he ever deserved it. It would be so undeserved we should call it "gratis," or free, or "grace."

There is a world of difference between being a creature of God and a child of God. We are *made* creatures of God; we *become* children of God by being reborn or begotten of Him. We are creatures because *made* by God. We make something that is *unlike* us, *e.g.*, a man makes a table. We beget something that is *like* us, for example, a father begets a child. When we receive this higher life inside us, we are not just *creatures* made by God, we become or are begotten something else. We are begotten as children of God, made partakers of His Divine Nature and heirs of the Kingdom of Heaven.

As beautiful as it is, there are not many who wish to receive that gift. Perhaps we can illustrate it by drawing a three-story house:

It has a basement, a first floor, and a second floor. This house looks like our house on 38th Street, except that we have to climb four flights of stairs for breakfast, lunch, and dinner. During Lent it is not worth it.

Some people *choose* to live in the basement, which corresponds to those who live a sensate existence. They think of themselves as animals, wanting only pleasures, never attempting to develop their minds or to perfect themselves culturally or artistically. If you told them there was another floor above that was much better and gave more happiness, they would say, "How do I know?" They never try to find out and thus miss many of the true joys of life.

The second floor is much better furnished and corresponds to the floor of art, science, and philosophy. Life is far more enjoyable here than in the basement of sensate existence. But if you tell these people there is another floor above the rational and the human which is more wonderfully furnished and gives greater happiness, that the radio and television there never have commercials, etc., they may answer, "I deny there is anything above me; I am all there is."

The deaf are dead to the great environment of sound and harmony; the blind are dead to the environment of beauty. So there are minds that are spiritually blind, in the sense that they are dead to the great environment of the Divine Who alone can give them peace of soul that surpasses all understanding. Nature *makes* man; this super-nature of grace *remakes* man. It is the latter whom William James rightly called the "twice-born."

Tremendous hidden reserves of power are available to anyone who desires them. But one must desire them. The door is opened only to him who knocks. The Divine only entreats, pleads, and offers, but He will not use force, even to save us from our shortsighted preference for a meaner and lower form of life. Some people refuse vaccination; some such people do not want to see a doctor; boys do not like to go to school, and man often refuses to be healed.

Happiness lies in the reach of him who would break the shell of egotism to contact this Divine world. To them is given to understand the words of Our Divine Lord, Who said, "How often would I have gathered thee to Myself, as the hen does gather her chicks."

CHAPTER EIGHTEEN

# The Psychology of the Irish

A previous telecast on the psychology of the Russian people produced many requests to say something about the Irish.

The three psychological traits of the Irish are:

1. Love of a fight.
2. Humor.
3. Blarney.

*Love of a fight.* It is sometimes said that people fight because they hate. It is just the contrary that is true. They fight because they love. The more a man loves, the more a man fights for what he loves. Loving God, they fight for their faith. Since the Irish believe also that there is more to love about Ireland than any other land, they fight more for it. No one fights for an abstraction. No swords are drawn in defense of relativity, but many a hand becomes a fist in defense of the Irish.

But a peculiar characteristic of Irish and fighting is that they also love to fight among themselves. If a little Jewish boy gets ahead—little Abie Cohen—all the Jewish boys say, "That's our Abie." But let Michael Rafferty get ahead and all the Irish start "knocking" Michael. This may be due to an excess of the democratic spirit, which regards everyone as equal. As soon as anyone sticks his head above the level of everyone, he gets hit with a blackthorn.

The real reason probably is deeper. Every Irishman believes himself to be a descendant of a king. There is not an O'Brien or a Farley or a Murphy who does not believe he descended from a king. Other people may believe they came from monkeys, but not the Irish. Since every Irishman once carried a scepter, why not carry a shillelagh? Since he once wore a crown, why should he not "crown"?

*Humor.* The amount of humor that anyone gets out of the world depends upon the size of the world in which he lives. Imagine the amount of humor available in the world as represented within arcs:

Obviously, if the only jokes we could tell were about mothers-in-law, the world would not be as laughable as if we could include jokes about the English. That would enlarge the area of humor considerably.

Suppose that, in addition to all the humor associated with time and this earth, we go beyond time to eternity, beyond earth to Heaven, from Broadway to the streets of gold—then one has an infinite reservoir from which to draw his humor. That is where the Irish principally draw their humor.

Here is an example: how the fairies came to Ireland. Ireland is peopled with fairies; no other people in the world seem to be interested in them except the Irish. But how did the fairies come to Ireland?

When Michael and Lucifer were having their great battle in Heaven, the smoke of battle finally cleared away. Banked against one of Heaven's blue clouds was a host of angels that had been doing no fighting whatever. They were under the leadership of a certain King O'Connor. It is difficult to believe that they were Irish angels and not in the fight, but that is the fact.

Archangel Gabriel was the first to see them; he went over to King O'Connor with righteous indignation, saying, "Almighty God has laid down the law that no one shall be crowned unless he has struggled. Instead of defending the rights of God, you have rested on your archangelic spear. If hell were not filled, I should cast you into it."

Archangel Michael came up, and this was said: "Listen,

Gabriel, don't be too hard on them. After all, they have not denied God, they merely have not fought."

And Gabriel said, "What can I do? An archangel cannot change his mind." (I believe that is theologically correct.) Archangel Michael answered, "God is going to make the earth soon; we will let King O'Connor and his angels make three wishes."

King O'Connor said, "I want to go to a land where there is gaming, fishing, sporting, and much laughter."

"Granted," said Michael.

"Second, I want to go to a land where the people are poor."

"Granted."

"And third, I want to go to a land where there is a Park Avenue."

Michael said, "No! You said you wanted to go where the people were poor."

And so the gates of Heaven were opened, and King O'Connor and his angels fell for 326 days, and they landed in Ireland, and they are the fairies of Ireland.

Associated with fairies are the little leprechauns. A leprechaun is about three inches high; sometimes he is a little shoemaker fairy. He hides in the bushes; if you look him straight in the eye, you make him a prisoner. To purchase his release, he grants you any three wishes you want. But you are not to tell anyone you saw the leprechaun.

This particular day, Bridget O'Toole was on her way to Mass; she looked in the hedges and there spied a leprechaun. She wanted some help with the wishes, so she went home to Michael her husband and said, "Michael, if you could have anything in all the world that you wanted, what would you want?"

There was a tinker going by selling lanterns. He said, "I wish I had one of those lanterns." Lo and behold! The lantern wafted into the home and suspended itself over the fireplace.

Bridget was so mad that, of all the fine castles of English lords he might have had, he chose a silly, stupid lamp; she said, "Glory be to God, I wish it were hanging from the end of your nose."

The lantern immediately began to swing from the end of Michael's nose, and she had to use the third wish to get it off, and then there weren't any wishes left.

That same sense of the invisible and the eternal gives the Irish their spiritual poetry in which earth tells of Heaven and the nature of Christ.

As Joseph Mary Plunkett writes in his poem "I See His Blood upon the Rose":

I see His blood upon the rose
  And in the stars, the glory of His eyes,
His body gleams amid eternal snows,
  His tears fall from the skies.

I see His face in every flower,
  The thunder and the singing of the birds
Are but His voice—and carven by His power
  Rocks are His written words.

All pathways by His feet are worn,
  His strong heart stirs the ever-beating sea,
His crown of thorns is twined with every thorn,
  His cross is every tree.

I remember an occasion when I recited that poem. It was some years ago at the Eucharistic Congress in Ireland. If there was ever a time in my life that I wanted to give a really fine oration, it was then. First of all, it was the Eucharistic Congress; and second, because it was in Ireland; and third, because my grandparents did not come from Bessarabia.

I was talking without any notes. Just before I decided to quote the poem, I threw out this line: "Ireland has never recognized any other king but Christ, and no other queen but Mary." You can imagine how the Irish liked that! Instead of paying attention to the poem I was reciting, I gave myself an intellectual spanking, saying to myself, "Now, no more cracks about kings and queens. This is the Eucharistic Congress; say nothing that can be misinterpreted politically, no matter how bright you think it is." I whipped myself so hard that when I reached the ninth line, "All pathways by His feet are worn," my mind went a complete and total blank.

I could not think of the last three lines. It was one of those blanks that we had during an examination in school—there is a finality about it; no use looking for the idea; it simply is not there. I stopped for what seemed like a minute, then said to the audience, "I am sorry, I have forgotten." I saw thousands of Irish jaws drop in disappointment, and when an Irish jaw drops, it collapses.

It is funny what comes to your mind in moments like these. What flashed across my mind was a line of Patrick Henry's—not the one that you know.

Patrick Henry also said something else in his life. He said,

"When you are in difficulty in an oration, throw yourself into the middle of a sentence, and trust God Almighty to get you to the other end."

So I did! I began, "I am glad I have forgotten." Of course, I really was not; but since I did not know what to say, I started over again. "If I have ever prayed to forget anything, I would have prayed to have forgotten these lines. There is beautiful symbolism in the forgetfulness. That symbolism is that, standing on the anvil of Ireland's soil, one should be able to hammer and forge out the sparks of his own poetry and not be dependent even on a magnanimous soul like Joseph Mary Plunkett."

When I had finished the oration, the chairman said, "Father Sheen, that was a wonderful trick of oratory, pretending that you forgot." It was too tragic to be a pretense.

*Blarney:* There is a difference between blarney and boloney. Blarney is the varnished truth; boloney is the unvarnished lie. Blarney is flattery laid on so thin you love it; boloney is flattery laid on so thick you hate it.

To tell a woman who is forty, "You look like sixteen," is boloney. The blarney way of saying it is "Tell me how old you are, I should like to know at what age women are most beautiful."

I once saw an Irishman get up in the subway and give his seat to a lady. She said, "You are a jewel."

He said, "Lady, I am a jeweler; I set jewels." That is blarney.

Blarney is always associated with imagination, which also seems a peculiar quality of the Irish. Those of you who have ever been down to Killarney probably met the boatmen there. Once I asked, "Is Killarney deep?"

"Deep? I had a nephew that dove in there six months ago. We got a post card from him in Australia last week. He wants his winter underwear."

I remember once being taken around Killarney by a charming driver. After the ride, I inquired how much I owed?

They never tell you, nor give you a direct answer. He said, "You know how it is! I have a wife and ten children."

So I gave him what was considered a fair rate and a really good tip. Whereupon he took off his coat, threw it over the horse's head, and said, "Father, I would be ashamed to let that horse see you giving me this."

I once had to resort to blarney on the occasion of a joint concert given by John McCormack and Grace Moore. On the way in, I met Lily McCormack (Mrs. John McCormack). She inquired where I would be seated in the theater. I said, "Up in the balcony."

"Come down and sit in my box."

So I went down to her box. John McCormack came out, sang a few songs, looked up to Lily, his wife, spotted me, and said, "Oh, I see we have Father Sheen in the audience. Let us have him come down and say a few words to you tonight."

I had no more business being on the stage of Carnegie Hall at a musical concert than I had playing in the Yankee infield.

What could you say on such an occasion? I resorted to a bit of blarney and told the story of John McCormack. "Some angels and some fairies assisted God in the making of the babe of Athlone. One of the angels went to the Shannon and stole from its waters the lilt. The fairies went down to Killarney, where on one side of the road the sun shines, and on the other side it rains, like a child that smiles through its tears and makes human rainbows. One took a ray of sunshine, the other a drop of rain.

"By fairy magic the ray of sunshine was converted into a smile and the drop of rain into a tear. The lilt and the smile and the tear were given to the babe of Athlone. The angel who stood nearby said, 'Oh, if he only had a voice, to articulate this lilt, this smile, and this tear. I shall go to Heaven and ask God for a voice.'

"God said, 'Over there in that corner of Heaven is a host of harps that have not been used since the day that Michael flashed his archangelic spear. Take from out one of those golden harps three golden chords, and string the throat of the babe of Athlone.'

"When the throat of the babe of Athlone had been strung with the golden chords from the golden harp of God, he cried. The angel said, 'Oh, how he will sing when he grows.'

"The fairies said, 'No man ever sings without an inspiration for a song.'

"The angel said, 'Where can we find it? Suppose we search for a flower that will be such an inspiration as to draw out all the melodies of that voice.'

"The angels and the fairies went down the East Coast and up the West, and finally they came to Dublin, where they found a beautiful Lily, and he has been singing to her ever since."

On the last day, when the Good Lord comes in the clouds of Heaven to judge the living and the dead, He will not show Himself to all people in just exactly the same way. Each people will see Him according to their own national characteristics.

I wonder, when He comes, if He will not seem to the Germans, who love pomp and circumstance, as a great King. Perhaps, He will show Himself to the Spaniards, who love the beauty of religion, with His Face shining as the sun and His garments white as snow. He will come to the people of India, who love mortification, showing scars on Hands and Feet and Side. But to the Irish, He will show something that He will show to no other people. He will show them His gratitude for their humor; He will show them His Smile!

## CHAPTER NINETEEN

# The Woman at the Well

In the garden of every heart goes on a great struggle, and only the soul and God know it. As planet affects planet, as the moon in some way moves all the surging tides of the world, so too every heart is stirred by influences of another world.

One of the most beautiful stories about a soul struggle is that of the woman at the well.

The place was Samaria, which is situated between Judea

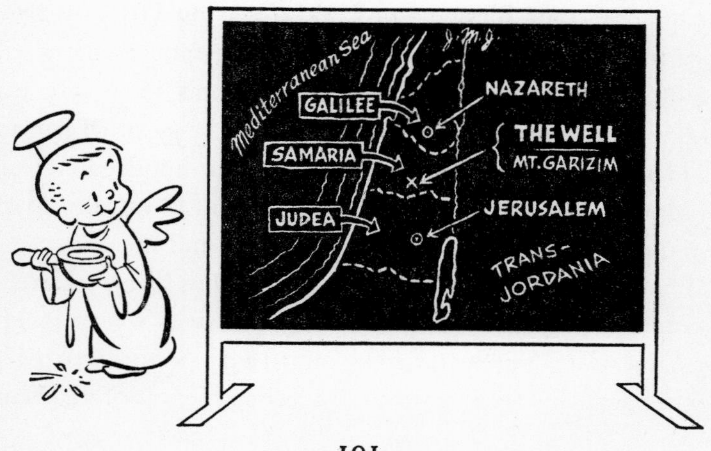

and Galilee. Galilee is the North; Judea is the South; Samaria is the middle.

The Good Samaritan as you may well guess came from Samaria. In the year 722 B.C. Assyria deported many from Samaria and also imported many Assyrians into Samaria. This intermingling of blood and religion produced a hybrid race—half Jewish and half Assyrian. The Samaritans built a temple of their own on Mount Garizim about the year 409 B.C. There was considerable enmity between the Jews and the Samaritans. The latter would often throw human bones into the Temple of Jerusalem in order to pollute it, thus stop the offering of religious rites. The Jew, for that reason, never liked to pass through Samaria when he went to Galilee. The Jews would light beacon fires on hilltops in order to let their people know, in another country, of the celebration of certain feasts. The Samaritans would light the fires two or three days ahead in order to confuse the Jews.

One day, Our Blessed Lord, Who was on His way from Judea to Galilee, did not avoid Samaria. He came near the village of Sichar and seated Himself at Jacob's Well. He was hungry and tired; far more hungering for the spiritual harvest was His Own Soul. Over against Him, eight hundred feet up, was Mount Garizim, where stood the ruins of the rival Samaritan temple. Behind Him, stood the Temple and the city.

The time of the day was noon, and Our Blessed Lord is described as weary from His journey. He was weary in His work, not of it. Weariness can be put to a purpose. Two of His most remarkable converts were made when He was tired. While

He sat at the well, a woman came to draw water. It was an unusual time to do so in Eastern countries, because of the heat. Generally, women come either in the morning or in the evening.

Our Blessed Lord began the conversation on the level of human necessity and asked her to give Him a drink. He knew her past history and her present life, but nevertheless He began by asking her to do Him a favor. Whenever God wishes to do us a favor, He often begins by asking for one. The purpose of His request is to create an emptiness in the heart. He, by Whom all things were made, the Creator of mountains and brooks and rivers, is not ashamed to ask a draught of water from the hand of one of His sinful creatures.

Her answer was "How is it that Thou, who art a Jew, dost ask me, a Samaritan, for a drink?"

Among us an enemy might ask and receive a drink of water without fear of compromising himself or his opponent; but not so in the East. There the giving and receiving of a drink of water is a covenant of hospitality.

Our Lord answered, "If thou knewest what it is God gives, and who this is saying to thee, 'Give me to drink' it would have been for thee to ask Him instead, and He would have given to thee Living Water."

The role of giver and seeker is reversed. The seeker becomes the giver; the giver, the seeker. Having asked for water, He sets forth the *Gift* under the image of water, as elsewhere, where men are waiting on Him for Bread, He sets forth the same "Gift" under the figure of Bread. He links the heavenly to the earthly and uses the earthly to explain the heavenly.

He speaks of three steps in coming to Him:

1. If thou knewest.
2. Thou wouldst have asked.
3. He would have given.

The first is knowledge—there is a touching reproach of her ignorance and bigotry, which blind so many. Before one can *ask,* one must *know.* The second step is desire: "Thou wouldst have asked." *Knowledge awakens appetite* and longing to possess; therefore, we must know God before we can want Him. It is our ignorance that fails to bring to our lips the cry "Give me to drink."

The third link in the chain is the giving. The asking must precede the giving. The gift is Himself. The Father does not give a creature or an angel or a seraph; He gives His Son. "God so loved the world that He gave His only begotten Son."

The woman saw the weary man, but not the Rest for weary souls; she saw the thirsty pilgrim, but not the One Who had quenched the world's thirst. The woman missed the deeper meaning of His speech. She took the figurative literally, and the spiritual, naturally. She now addressed Him with some courtesy, calling Him "Sir," and then added, "Thou hast nothing to draw with and the well is deep. From whence then hast Thou Living Water?"

She proceeded with the intention of showing that these pretensions of His involved an absurdity. We may suppose the woman held the bucket in her own hand while she talked with Our Lord and reminded Him that He had nothing of the kind.

The natural man considers spiritual things in a carnal way and thus misses God's gift. The woman thought Our Lord was speaking of elementary water.

The woman then covered the possibility that He might have discovered another well as she asked, "Art Thou greater than our father Jacob who gave us this well and drank thereof and his children and his cattle?"

Our Blessed Lord did not entangle Himself in a direct reply to the question "Art Thou greater than our father Jacob?" but He implicitly did give a reply. "Whosoever drinketh of this water shall thirst again; whosoever drinketh of the water that I shall give him shall never thirst. The water I give him will be a spring of water within him, that flows continually to bring him everlasting life."

What is to take the place of the world's broken cistern? You cannot dislodge one object of the world's earthly affection without the substitution of something better. Nature abhors a vacuum. Our Lord does not condemn earthly streams or forbid them. He merely says, "You will never be satisfied." The believer has an inner well in his soul which, too, must have its Water. Earthly water never rises above its own level, and so the best of earthly thrills and pleasures can rise no higher than the earth. They begin and end there. The Living Water with which Christ fills the soul, springing from Heaven, leads to Heaven again. Flowing from the Infinite, it elevates to the Infinite, finds its level in the river of the water of life which flows in the midst of celestial Paradise.

There was a certain blind longing awakened in the soul

of the woman who had thirsted so long and who already had slaked her thirst at one of the muddiest pools of sensual gratification. She exclaimed, "Sir, give me water such as that, so that I may never be thirsty and have to come here for water again." She could not understand the miraculous Water, but she thought possibly she could be spared from walking out at noon, a mile and a half, to draw water.

It could very well be that she expected to receive this Water without any effort at all, which would account for the words which Our Blessed Lord addressed to her next. "Go home, fetch thy husband, and come back here."

The words can only be regarded as spoken for the calling out of that very answer which they did call out, namely, the bringing her to wholesome shame. They attained the object for which they were uttered—her confession of guilt. The conviction of sin is the beginning of the great work of the spirit.

"I have no husband." Jesus answered, "True enough, thou hast no husband. Thou hast had five husbands, but the man who is with thee now is no husband of thine; thou hast told the truth over this."

Our Lord's condemnation of the woman's honest confession teaches that we should make the best of an ignorant sinner's words. An unskillful physician of souls would probably have rebuked the woman sharply for her wickedness, but Our Lord said, "Thou hast told the truth over this."

She had asked for Living Water; she knew not that the well must first be dug, that hard clay needs to be removed. "Go home, fetch thy husband," is the first stroke summoning her to repentance.

How would you like someday to be at a fountain, and have somebody come along and make a statement about your divorces, and the man you were now living with? What would you do? You would do exactly what she did. It is not only the women that would do it; every man would do the same thing. *She changed the subject.* She said, "Sir, I perceive that thou art a prophet." The woman was making a wild attempt to get off the hook. Our Lord was now beginning, in her opinion, to meddle. Conversion is in the moral order. The woman would make it solely intellectual. She wanted religion to be a matter of discussion, when the Saviour was making it one of decision. She had been compelled to own up, so she adopted a method of raising a theological point.

"Well, it was our fathers' way to worship on this mountain, although you tell us that the place where men ought to worship is in Jerusalem."

She was now drawing Him off some unwelcome truths about her life, and she introduced a doctrinal problem; thus she would avoid shame to herself.

Our Lord answered, "Believe me, woman, the time is coming when you will not go to this mountain, nor yet to Jerusalem, to worship the Father. You worship you cannot tell what, we worship knowing what it is we worship; salvation, after all, is to come from the Jews; but the time is coming, nay, has already come, when the true worshipers will worship the Father in spirit and in truth; such men as these the Father claims for his worshipers."

The Blessed Trinity is here implied, for there is the Father, the Spirit, Which is the Holy Ghost, and the Truth, Which is the Son Who speaks with the woman. God the Father has not always been so worshiped. Christ has come to reveal Him as such. He reveals Him not just as Creator, Who made the mountain and the insects, but as One Who communicates an existence like His own. Worship must take its character from the Nature of God, and not from the nature of any people or nation or race. Almost all attempts at religious unity start with man instead of with God the Father. All who are looking for the unity of religion must not start whittling away the Divine Truths. Rather, as He said, "Start at the top; get the right understanding of God, then you will be one."

When He said, "The time is coming," she said, "I know the Christ is coming; and when He comes, He will tell us everything." Can you imagine the surprise of that woman when this chance passerby at the well said to her, "I, Who speak to thee, am the Christ"? All the longings of thousands of years, of the poets, philosophers, and dramatists—Virgil, Sophocles, Buddha, Confucius, Moses—all of them were pointing to this hour when He said, "I am the Christ. . . . I am the Teacher of the Truth; I am the Son of That Father."

She was so amazed at what she heard that she ran into the city and left her water bucket at the well. Maybe she forgot it; maybe she left it as a symbol that she no longer wanted earthly water. Now we come to an interesting part of the story.

Why was that woman at the well at the noon hour to draw water? Because she was that kind of woman; she was a public woman, and other women would not allow her to associate with them.

She ran into the city. She told the men; she got even with the gossiping women. She had found the Teacher, and she told only the men. A few hours later, picture this woman coming out of the city; trailing behind her are the men of Samaria; she was leading them now along the right ways, when she once led them along evil ways. They turned out to be rather an ungrateful lot, for they finally said to her, "It is not through thy report that we believe now; we have heard Him for ourselves, and we recognize that He is indeed the Saviour of the world."

They invited Him into their own village, out of which for the first time, in the hearing of the world, came the great title that He bears preeminently, the title given by the woman at the well, and the men and women of the city, the glorious title—Saviour of the world!

## CHAPTER TWENTY

# Pain and Suffering

Our capacity for pain is greater than our capacity for pleasure. Suffering reaches the point where we feel we can endure it no longer, and yet it increases and we endure it. But pleasures very quickly reach a peak and then begin a decline. Age decreases the capacity for pleasures. Though pain never turns into a pleasure, a pleasure can turn into a pain. Tickling may be funny at first, but it can also become excruciatingly painful. Our capacity for pain is greater because the Good Lord intended that all pain should be exhausted in this world. The Divine Plan is to have real joys in the next life.

Because so many in our world suffer anxieties that grow like fire or a loneliness that spreads like a desert or else experience heartaches, disappointments, bereavements, and scorpion thrusts of pain, we thought it fitting to say something of the philosophy of suffering and evil.

Our subject will be divided into three parts:

1. What pain or suffering does to us.
2. How to meet it.
3. Why there is suffering.

The first effect of pain is that it makes us concentrate on ourselves. A toothache creates a barrier between us and the outside world; pain makes us so attentive to the ego as to kill our social instincts. If you have the colic, it is hard to be altruistic. We often invoke our sickness as an excuse for our selfishness, egotism, and impatience. But this concentration on the ego can be "for better or for worse," just like marriage. I was going to say something about this analogy, but I will not. A very good rule on television is "Always think before you speak, then talk to yourself."

As Franz Werfel expressed it, "Sickness invites us to heaven or to hell." It invites us to hell, and makes us worse, when it intensifies selfishness; it makes us bitter and disgruntled, or tyrants demanding constant attention. Such is the tyranny of sickness. Some persons in hospitals are constantly ringing for a nurse. As W. C. Fields once put it, "They take a turn for the nurse."

Sickness can also liberate a man from his selfishness and so transform his soul as to reveal the mystery of his being. At least one thing pain can do is to cut down the opportunities for sinning and thus prepare the soul for virtue; it also gives one an opportunity to study himself, to examine his conscience, to inquire into the purpose of life. Sickness prevents many a man from being a scoundrel and gives him a chance to mend his ways. Many a man who is a sinner is unable to sin when he is flat on his back. There is much more opportunity for sinning when one is well than when one is ill.

Once offered as a sacrifice, pain can liberate the soul and

turn a curse into a blessing. This "better or worse" quality of pain finds its two most perfect examples in the two thieves who were crucified on Calvary on either side of Our Divine Lord. Actually, there seems to have been no difference between these two thieves, at the beginning. They were sentenced for the same crime; they were both equally criminal; they both blasphemed; they both suffered crucifixion. Then something happened. Pain forced them to concentrate on the ego. The thief on the left became worse. Pain, unsanctified, can sear, spoil, and scorch the soul. The thief on the left asked to be taken down. "Save Thyself, and us too, if Thou art the Christ." He wanted to be taken down in order that he might go on with the dirty, sordid business of stealing.

The thief on the right, though he began with cursing, soon saw his own pains as the just reward of his sins and protested against the gibes of his brother thief. "Hast thou no fear of God, when thou art undergoing the same sentence? And we justly enough; we receive no more than the due reward of our deeds; but this man has done nothing amiss."

Then he turned to Our Lord and said, "Remember me when Thou comest into Thy kingdom." The answer came back, "I promise thee, this day thou shalt be with me in Paradise." "Thou"—it was the affirmation of democracy, the declaration of the worth of a single individual. That thief died a "thief," for he stole Paradise. Paradise can be stolen again!

The next question related to pain is *how to meet it*. There are actually three solutions about pain. One is the Stoic solution, which is to grit your teeth and bear it. The second is the

Buddhist, which holds that all pain and suffering come from desire. If we could extinguish all our desires, we would eventually reach a point of tranquillity where we would be absorbed into the great Nirvana of unconsciousness. The third solution is the Hebraic-Christian philosophy of pain, which believes that pain and suffering can be transcended.

Suffering is transcended through love. Pain without love is suffering or hell. Suffering with love is sacrifice. Love does not have the power to kill pain or to extinguish it, but it does have the power to diminish it. After losing money, a person often says, "I hope some poor person found it." The love of the poor softens the loss. A mother sits up all night with a fever-stricken child, but it is not suffering to her; it is love and sacrifice. No work is hard where there is love. Students who do not love a subject never do well in that subject. If then we can bear so much out of human love, how much more patient will we be out of love for God. As a father sometimes gives bitter medicine to his child, so, too, the Heavenly Father gives it for some greater good. We know that somehow a cross fits into the plan and purpose of this sinful world; otherwise He would not have allowed His Divine Son to be crucified.

Never losing our love of God, we can then find reasons for supporting pain. If we have ruined our health by excesses, we impose upon ourselves dietary laws and avoid delicacies out of love for our health. One can do the same with the soul. One can say, "I will accept this particular suffering in order to make reparation for my own faults." Or we can also offer up our suffering for others. We live in a universe in which we help other people. Though some wear the best of Forstmann's woolens, they did not raise the sheep; they share in the labors of other sheep. Most of us do not raise the vegetables that we eat. We share in the communion of workers. So we can transfer and communicate to others the merits of our sufferings, offered in union with the Cross.

Doctors will graft skin from one part of the body to the face, if the face is burned. Those suffering from anemia receive a transfusion of blood from another member of society to cure them of that disease. If it is possible to transfuse blood, it is also possible to transfuse sacrifice. If it is possible to graft skin, it is also possible to graft prayer. We have blood banks for our own soldiers, that their lives may be saved through our sacrifice of blood. Pain, agony, disappointments, injustices—all these can be poured into a heavenly treasury from which the anemic, sinful, confused, ignorant souls may draw unto the healing of their wings.

Thus through love of God suffering becomes sacrifice. The great mystery of the world is not what people suffer; it is what they miss when they suffer! They could be minting coinage for their own salvation and the salvation of the world. The tragedy of wasted pain! The unsanctified tears! The dull aches, the nauseating pains, the infuriating doublecrosses! How much of these are wasted and thereby converted into curses, because those who suffer them have no One to love! Life may be like a game of cards; we cannot help the hand that is dealt us, but we can help the way we play it. The lovelessness of lives is always the fault of a soul; the pain of life is not always such. The secret is to bring our little crosses under the shadow of the Cross, "Whom Love made life, Life made pain, and Pain made death."

That brings us to our final question, and, of course, I cannot give the complete answer to the why of pain and suffering. One of the very best stories of the problem of suffering is contained in the Hebraic tradition in the Old Testament in the Book of Job. Job was a very wealthy man who lived in a large house with much land. He had seven sons and three daughters. He had thousands and thousands of oxen, sheep, and camels, and every one of his children had a country home.

The Sabeans came in and took his oxen; the Chaldeans came and stole his camels. Lightning struck his sheep; lightning struck the house of the eldest son, and he was killed. Then Job finally developed some ailment which covered him with sores from head to foot. His answer was that the Lord gave and the Lord takes away; "praised be the Lord."

His wife could not understand anybody who could say that, and she said, "Curse God and die." Poor Job, in addition to all his troubles, had the worry of a troublesome wife.

You know what that reminds me of? You know the Trappists do not speak, and they have various signs for "today," "tomorrow," "next week." You know what the sign for "woman" is? It is pounding the forehead with the fist.

Well, getting back to Job—Job had some comforters, and they came to see and console him. They first sat for seven days, according to oriental custom, saying nothing.

Here was poor Job, whose wife would not allow him in the

house, seated on a dunghill, cleaning his sores. After seven days, his comforters began to speak, and their solutions all boiled down to this: "Job, do you know why you are suffering? It is because you are not leading a good life." They were saying that there is an equation between economics and piety, and there are many who believe that. "So Job, if you are no longer prosperous, it must mean that you are no longer pious."

Job was not conscious of any sin, and Job rebelled against that suggestion, and rightly so. But Job did not know the answer either, and he began to ask himself many questions. "Why this loss; why this suffering; why this pain; why was I ever born; why was I ever nestled at my mother's breast; why did I ever see the light of day?" He yearned that God might come and answer all of his questions.

Suppose the Book of Job stopped there. What a wonderful opportunity for a Broadway drama! Here is Job, suffering, asking all of these questions, and a Broadway dramatist would have made God walk across the stage and say, "Job, what are your questions?" God would answer them all, and the universe would clear.

And yet the Divine Dramatist does not operate that way. Actually, out of the whirlwind does come the voice of God, and God speaks and He says, "Strip, then, and enter the lists; it is my turn to ask questions now, thine to answer them. From what vantage-point wast thou watching, when I laid the foundations of the earth? Tell me, since thou art so wise, was it thou or I designed earth's plan, measuring it out with the line? How came its base to stand so firm, who laid its corner-stone? Was it thou or I shut in the sea behind bars? No sooner had it broken forth from the womb than I dressed it in swaddling-clothes of dark mist, set it within bounds of my own choosing, made fast with bolt and bar; Thus far thou shalt come, said I, and no further; here let thy swelling waves spend their force. Tell me if such knowledge is thine, all its secrets; where the light dwells, where darkness finds its home; hast thou followed either of these to the end of its journey, tracked it to its lair? Didst thou foresee the time of thine own birth, couldst thou foretell the years of life that lay before thee? What sire gendered the rain, or the drops of dew; what mother's womb bore the ice, the frost that comes from heaven to make water hard as stone, imprison the depths beneath its surface? Dost thou tell the day-star when to shine out, the evening star when to rise over the sons of earth? Can thy voice reach the clouds, and bid their showers fall on thee; canst thou send out lightnings that will do thy errand, and come back to await thy pleasure? What power gives either man's heart its prescience, or the cock its sure instinct, knows all the motions of heaven, and lulls the music of the spheres?"

And thus Job made the Lord answer: "So vain a pleader, I have no suit to make; finger on lip I will listen."

The intelligence of Job was nothing compared with the mind of God, just as the mouse in the piano would never understand why anyone should sit down and play the keys of a piano. As the brain of a mouse is below that of man, so is the brain of man below the mind of God.

Finally, Job had everything restored to him sevenfold, because God never closes His door but that He also opens the window. That still did not quite answer the question because people might still ask, "Yes, but is there not such a thing as sacrifice in the world?" How do you explain that?

I tell you that if God in Heaven had not come down to this earth in the form of a man, and given us the supreme example of sacrifice, then it would be possible for fathers and mothers, men and women of countless ages, to do something greater, it would seem, than God Himself could do, namely, lay down their lives for a friend.

Once He came, then never again could they say, "He does not know what it is like to suffer." He walked through the forest first and made the pathway and showed us that without Good Friday there would be no Easter Sunday. Never again can anyone say, "What have I done to deserve this?"

He could ask from the Cross, "What have I done to deserve this?"

When there is a murder mystery, you never walk out because the hero is killed in the first act. It is the last act that crowns the play. To be His captive is to be free.

> I slipped His fingers, I escaped His feet,
> I ran and hid, for Him I feared to meet.
> One day I passed Him, fettered on a Tree.
> He turned His head, looked, and beckoned me.
>
> Neither by speed, nor strength could He prevail.
> Each hand and foot was pinioned by a nail,
> He could not run and clasp me if He tried,
> But with His eye, He bade me reach His side.
> For pity's sake thought I, I'll set you free.
> 'Nay—hold this cross,' He said, 'and follow Me.'
> 'This yoke is easy, this burden light,
> Not hard or grievous if you wear it tight.'
> So did I follow Him Who could not move,
> An uncaught captive in the hands of Love.

CHAPTER TWENTY-ONE

# Comparison of the Soviet and the American Constitutions

Any good citizen, if asked by Congress if he were a member of Murder, Inc., would immediately deny it. Why is it, then, that some of our citizens insist on their constitutional rights when asked if they are Communists? It will help all citizens and in particular those who are reluctant to affirm their loyalty to their country, to make a comparison of the Soviet and the American Constitutions. The comparison will consider:

1. The remote origin of power.
2. The proximate source of rights and liberties.
3. The extent of rights and liberties.

1. *The origins.* What is the ultimate source of political power? According to our Constitution and the Declaration of Independence, the source of our rights is God. According to the Soviet Constitution, Article I, the ultimate origin of power is the "Socialist state."

The second paragraph of our Declaration of Independence tells us where we get our basic rights and liberties. Our Founding Fathers were concerned with that problem. They had to ask whence these rights and liberties came. Did they come from the will of the majority? If they came from the will of the majority, then the will of the majority could take away the rights of the minority. In a democracy, the majority is the custodian of minority rights. If our rights came from the state, the state could take them away. They set down the source of rights in the second paragraph, writing: "We hold these truths to be self-evident, that all men are created equal, that they are endowed by their Creator with certain inalienable Rights, that among these are Life, Liberty, and the pursuit of happiness."

In the Soviet Constitution, if there are any rights, they come from the Socialist state. Note the difference! If rights come to us from God, then no state, no parliament, no dictator can ever take them away! If they come from the Socialist state, then the Socialist state can take them away. This is the fundamental difference between the two. For us, the state exists for the person; for the Soviets, the person for the state. For us, a person has rights independent of the state; for the Soviet, no rights are inalienable; they can all be dispossessed by the state that gave them.

2. *The proximate source of right.* In what do our rights and liberties reside? According to us, they reside in the *person;* according to the Soviet, in the *class.* There is a difference between the person and the class: A person is a being with a rational soul and, therefore, has rights. A pig has no rational soul and, therefore, has no rights. A flower has no soul and, therefore, no rights. A baby has a soul and, therefore, has in-

alienable rights, even though the baby cannot express its desire to live. Rights do not depend on utility or social welfare, but on the soul itself. Abortion is wrong because if the soul is there, there is a person. Is "unmerciful killing" wrong? (Some call it "mercy killing," but since killing is murder, it is unmerciful.) Unmerciful killing is wrong because a person has a soul that came from God. Not only may we not kill the aged or our political opponents; we may not even kill those who recommend unmerciful killing. For us, their rights come from God.

In the last century, some political centers said that rights came to us from society. But if rights come to us from society, then society can destroy them. John Stuart Mill said that the reason we have rights and liberties is because they are useful for society. That was a very dangerous thing to say, because he made rights dependent upon social welfare, and not inherent in the person. Granted utility as the basis of rights, it will not be long before someone will come along and say, "Maybe it is not useful for an individual to have any rights at all." That is precisely what Karl Marx said, who was the founder of Communism. He then put all rights in the revolutionary class, and not in the person made to the image and likeness of God, as we do.

Karl Marx understood better than even some in America the inherent source of right. Marx did not like democracy because he said that democracy is founded on a principle that every man has a soul, independently of any society or class. Marx said, "I contend that only the class has rights. *An individual has no value whatever unless he is a member of the revolutionary class.*"

3. *Extent of rights.* How many rights do we have in the United States Constitution and how many in the Soviet? Our Constitution does not limit rights; the Soviet Constitution does; it grants none, except those mentioned in the Constitution.

Amendment IX of our Bill of Rights states, "The enumeration in the Constitution of certain rights shall not be construed to deny or disparage others retained by the people." The extent of our rights and liberties is not limited by the Constitution. Here Amendment IX goes back to the Declaration of Independence—God gave us inalienable rights before there was a Constitution; therefore, we have other rights than those mentioned in the Bill of Rights.

In the Soviet Constitution, you go through 9 chapters, 117 articles, setting up an absolute, totalitarian, monolithic, materialistic state before you come to the mention of a single right! After waiting all this time, wading through all this Communist double talk, you are naturally full of expectancy to see what will be the first right. What do you think it is? The right to work! Not even the right to life.

There are only six rights mentioned in the Soviet Constitution. There are a few others that are "recognized" on certain conditions.

It is interesting to compare the Soviet Constitution translated into English by the Communists and the same Soviet Constitution translated into English and published here in the United States by a certain peace foundation. We shall not name it. It uses the word "guaranteed rights" when all the Soviet Constitution says is "recognized on certain conditions."

Thus the Communist fellow travelers are more generous to the Soviet Constitution than are the Communists themselves.

Some years ago, we were discussing the Constitution with a Communist. We mentioned that there was no right acknowledged until we came to Article 118. He answered by quoting an almanac well known in this country. We were arguing about the Soviet Constitution. We quoted the Constitution, and he came back with an almanac. We told him about a young wife who came home one evening and found her husband seated under a lamp with a small book in his hand. The wife said, "What are you reading?"

He said, "I am reading an almanac."

She went into her bedroom, threw herself on the bed, and began to cry. Her mother came in—her mother lived with them—and asked, "Child, what is wrong?"

The daughter raised herself from the pillow, tears streaming down her cheeks, and said, "Ma, I've married a bookworm."

The first right of all in the Soviet Constitution is Article 118, the right to work. How about the right *not to work?* In other words, how about the *right to strike?* It would be most striking to find that in the Soviet Constitution. Naturally it is not there. But what is still worse is that Article 131 regards all strikers as "enemies of the people." The Communists tell our American workers that they are working for exploiters. Maybe a few are, but employers are not all exploiters. Even if they were, at least in the United States a man can go from one exploiter to another. But when the state is the only exploiter, as in Russia, you can go nowhere else, except to Siberia.

Article 118, or the right to work, is followed by the curious Article 119, in which, with pontifical solemnity, the Soviet Constitution grants to its citizens the same inherent rights that God has given to the bees and the fleas and the monkeys, namely, the "right to rest."

Once in a discussion with a Communist fellow traveler, he argued, "We do not have the right to rest in the American Constitution."

I said, "Of course not! The reason we do not have it is because we do not receive all of our rights from the Constitution. They are inherent and they come to us from God, and if the Constitution did not give us the right to rest, *we would take it anyway*."

Consider next the freedom of religion and the right to adore God according to the dictates of conscience. Amendment I of our Bill of Rights states that "Congress shall make no law respecting an establishment of religion, or prohibiting the free exercise thereof." Let it be stated clearly and absolutely that we are proud of that amendment; we want it to stay in our Constitution. I know of no one who is working for any established church that would contravene Amendment I of our Constitution.

We have to wait until Article 124 of the Soviet Constitution to hear anything about religion. Here a distinction between worship and propaganda is made. Article 124 reads, "Freedom of religious *worship* and freedom of anti-religious *propaganda* are recognized for all of the citizens." "Freedom of worship" is recognized if you can find a church. The Communists closed 52,000 of them and liquidated the clergy.

May you preach religion? May you broadcast religion? May you publish tracts on religion? *No.* That is *propaganda*, and the Constitution states that the right of antireligious propaganda belongs to the Soviets, but the right to propagate the Faith does not exist in Communist Russia.

The basis of this Soviet objection to religious freedom is obvious. Communism is totalitarianism. Totalitarianism means the *total* possession of man: *body and soul.* A democracy leaves the soul free to serve its God. But totalitarianism cannot afford to allow the soul to be free. Hence it must persecute religion. Where the soul is, there is liberty. Ice has no spirit; it *must* be cold. To extinguish liberty, totalitarianism must persecute the soul. The exile of God always means the tyrannization of man.

Next, consider freedom of press and speech. Amendment I of our Constitution speaks of freedom of the press and the right to petition the government for redress of grievances. Article 125 of the Soviet Constitution states that the Soviet recognizes freedom of the press, freedom of assembly, freedom of speech for all of its citizens—here comes the *catch*—"on condition that they are used to support the Soviet Socialist system." Suppose you do not want to use your press to support Communism? Suppose you want to talk against Communism? Then you have no freedom.

Another comparison centers around elections. We have free elections in this country. The people may nominate candidates;

they may also use a secret ballot to elect their government officials. Article 141 of the Soviet Constitution states that the Communist party alone has the right to nominate candidates. There is only one party in Russia, and that is the Communist party. It represents only 3 per cent of the population. Their elections are therefore nothing else than an experiment for putting a cheer in writing. The lever in the election booth only goes one way—*down* to a Communist!

It may be interesting, too, to recall that on October 23, 1934, Molotov expressed in *Izvestia* the Soviet attitude toward forced elections: "In the Communist election, no one will dare show his nose except Communists because our dictatorship strikes without pity."

On November 13, 1937, the Russian publication *Trud* stated, "The sole possibility with Communism is this: one party is in power, and all the rest are in jail."

Finally, one of the great differences between our Constitution and that of the Soviet is that ours established a government of the people; theirs established a government of the masses.

People are persons. A person is a rational being who is self-determined, has his own conscience and a personality that is unique and incommunicable, and is a source of inalienable rights and liberties.

Who are the masses? They are persons who have lost their consciences; they are persons who are not self-determined but are moved from the outside by propaganda; they are like ants in an anthill of the Soviet state. The masses are not the opposite of class, but the opposite of personality. They have been so "brain-washed" that they are susceptible to every form of mental contagion, are profoundly imitative and ready to believe anything that is repeated often enough.

The grave danger in democracy is that the people may become the masses. Our government is not the government of the masses. Our Constitution begins, "We the *people* of the United States . . . do ordain and establish this Constitution for the United States of America."

Lincoln, in his Gettysburg address, echoed our glorious Constitution, in expressing his hope that "government of the *people*, by the *people*, and for the *people*" might not perish from the earth.

We are people because we are persons; we are persons because we have souls; because we have souls, we have rights, and these rights came to us from God. If we wish to keep our perfume, we must keep our flowers; if we wish to keep our forests, we must keep our trees; if we wish to keep our rights, we must also keep our God!

## CHAPTER TWENTY-TWO

# Not As Queer As We Think

The popularity of psychiatry has made many normal people worry about their mental condition. Be consoled! You are not as queer as you think.

A few people may be queer. For example, the woman who was suing for higher alimony. She told the judge that she needed twenty-four new frocks a month. The judge said to her, "What could a woman possibly want with twenty-four new frocks?"

Her answer was, "Twenty-four new hats."

There are various degrees of queerness, oddness, and eccentricity. If you are poor, you are "crazy"; if you are rich, you have an "Oedipus complex." Fifteen years ago I heard this explanation given by a husband who was told by the doctor, "I am afraid that your wife is losing her mind."

The husband answered, "I should not be a bit surprised; she has been giving me a piece of it every day for the last fifteen years."

We begin as usual with a distinction that is a trifle technical, but very important. It is the distinction between *nature* and *person*. This piece of chalk has a nature; but it is not a person.

A nature is a principle of activity—the chalk is capable of acting, of writing. A person, however, is a source of responsibility. The chalk is not responsible for the poor drawings. A cow has a nature, but a cow is not a person. A cow has no rights.

Nature furthermore is something that is common to many. For example, we speak of human nature, or humanity. The person, however, is concrete, individual. In a certain sense it is incommunicable. No one else but George Washington has ever had George Washington-ness.

As we talk of eccentricities and tensions, we are not concerned here with what is personal, although a person can accentuate certain tensions which are found in human nature. We are concerned only with that which is found universally, in all human natures—tensions that belong to Chinese, to Japanese, to Americans, to English, in a word, to the human race.

Now, the tensions that are common to human nature can be reduced to three:

1. Anxiety.
2. Contradiction.
3. Temptation.

*Anxiety*. Everyone feels within himself a pull between his desires for infinite happiness and the finite, limited happiness he actually attains. The basis of all disappointment is the disproportion between what we imagine *or wish for* to make us happy and what we actually possess. We can imagine a mountain of gold in our backyard, but we never see one.

This tension is inherent in every human nature, because on

the one hand the soul craves the infinite and the body, on the other hand, is "cabined, cribbed, confined" to the material and temporal. Each of us feels like a mountain climber whose happiness consists in reaching the heights above but, at the same time, is always threatened by a fall into the depths below. Suspended between the two, he yearns for an ideal but knows within his heart he can fall away from it.

*Contradiction.* Everyone feels himself a mixture of good and evil. As Ovid put it, "I see and approve the better things of life, the worse things of life I follow." The pleasures of the body are not always the delights of the soul; sometimes they are contrary to one another. The lusts of the flesh militate against the aspirations of the spirit. To be happy on the inside, one ought to make the body subject to the soul, but what is "immoral, unlawful or fattening" does not easily surrender to the will. One feels sometimes that he is driving a team of horses: one horse is pulling in one direction, the other horse is pulling in the other direction. Goethe regretted that God made only one man of him because there was enough in him to make a rogue and a gentleman. "Dr. Jekyll and Mr. Hyde" is to some extent the story of Everyman, who can say of himself: [1]

> Within my earthly temple there's a crowd:
> There's one of us that's humble, one that's proud;
> There's one that's broken-hearted for his sins
> And one who unrepentant sits and grins;
> There's one who loves his neighbor as himself,
> And one who cares for naught but fame and pelf.

[1] From *A Little Brother of the Rich, and Other Verse* by Edward Sanford Martin (Charles Scribner & Sons).

From much corroding care I should be free,
If once I could determine which is me.

*Temptation.* Oscar Wilde said, "I can resist anything but temptation." A temptation is often a suppressed evil which combats the good. This illustration pictures a cellar in which there are many little temptations, which we shall call "bad angels" or "little devils," though they are not necessarily such.

The stairs lead from the lower self, or cellar, to the higher self, or the soul and the things of God. Here is one little devil who is already going up the stairs. At the top of the stairs is a door which admits to the will which decides whether or not the temptation will succeed. In the cellar are many kinds of temptations, though they are principally three: pride, lust, greed. One little devil is the "knock-his-block-off" devil. When anybody says anything nasty to you, or steps on your toes, the little devil always says, "Hit him back."

Another little devil is the divorce devil. As soon as a husband and wife quarrel, this little devil says, "Go home to mother" or "Let's get a divorce."

The little sex devils talk this way: "After all, we are descended from animals, aren't we? And if we came from beasts, we ought to act like beasts, shouldn't we? Go ahead, you live only once."

Conscience and the human will try to drive out these temptations from the mind. At this point, it is extremely important to keep in mind that a person is not bad because he has a temptation. Many believe, because they have a temptation to pride, to avarice, to hate, to lust, that there is something wrong with them. There is nothing wrong with you if you are tempted. You are not tempted because you are evil; you are tempted because you are *human*. There is nothing intrinsically evil about human nature just because a little devil knocks at the door. Evil begins only when we open the door and consent to the temptation. Scripture praises the man who suffers temptations. When we resist temptations, we strengthen our character.

To sum it up, human nature has various tensions such as the pull of the infinite, the contradiction between what we *ought* to be and what we *are*, and finally the temptation to fall away from our ideals. This is human nature, and we must accept it as such. We are not as queer as we think we are.

The problem is how to explain why our human nature acts this way. Some great psychologists have given the following explanations:

*William McDougall* suggests the distinction between *nature* and *person* and holds that something is in human nature independent of the persons which compose the human race. "The aggregate which is society, has, in virtue of its past history, *positive qualities* which it does *not derive from the units* which compose it at any one time. . . ."

*Carl Jung* says that there is a substratum or a kind of river in which every person bathes who becomes a member of the human race. This substratum he calls "collective unconsciousness." "I am so profoundly convinced of this homogeneity of the human psyche, that I have actually embraced it in the concept of the collective unconscious. It is a *universal* and homogeneous *substratum* whose homogeneity extends into a world-wide identity."

If this tension that is in us refers to something way back in the beginning of our history, we must discount the idea that it is totally personal in origin. If the tension were personal in origin, not every person would have it. It may be intensified by the person, but it is not created by him.

Nor is it animal in origin, because no animal has a psychosis. A chicken never has an Electra complex. It takes the spirit to make a man either hope or despair. Human nature is not intrinsically wicked. It is rather disordered, just like a fish out of water, or like a clock whose mainspring is broken. The intellect is darkened to some extent, but it still knows truth; the will is weakened to some extent, but it still can love the good. The tension has all the appearance of resulting from a free moral act, the effects of which affect human nature and which, according to these psychologists, seem to have been transmitted through humanity.

Music offers us some explanation of what might have happened at the beginning of the human race. An orchestra director has before him his score. It was written by a great composer, and all the adequate directions have been scored for a perfect rendition. The musicians are all free; they can follow the directions of the conductor, or they can ignore them. They can be either reactionary and never turn a page, or they can be liberal and play, instead of the symphony, "I Got Plenty of Nothin'."

Now suppose that one of the musicians decides deliberately to hit a sour note. The conductor hears it. He may either wave his baton and order the orchestra to play it over, or he can ignore it. It makes no difference which he does, because, at a certain temperature, that note is flying out into space at the rate of 1,200 feet a second. As long as time endures, there is discord and disharmony somewhere in God's universe.

Regardless of how much one wanted to make the universe universally harmonious again, it could not be done by anyone within time, because time is irreversible.

The only way that discord could be stopped would be by someone reaching out from eternity, laying hold of that wild note, and stopping it in its mad flight. But would it still be a sour note? Not necessarily. On one condition it could become a sweet note, namely, if the one who stopped it wrote a new symphony and made that one note the first note in the new melody. Then it would be a sweet note.

Something like that must have happened at the beginning of the human race. God wrote a perfect symphony. It was well scored, but mankind was free to play a discord. Discords in the symphony of life did not mean our freedom was destroyed.

At the beginning, man being free hit a discordant note, a disobedient note. That discord went through human nature, and it infected everyone. That original discord could not be stopped by man himself, because he could not repair an offense against the infinite with his finite self. He had contracted a bigger debt than he could pay. The debt could be paid only by the Divine Master Musician coming out of His Eternity into time. But there is a world of difference between stopping a discordant note and a rebellious man. One has no freedom, the other has; and God refuses to be a totalitarian dictator in order to abolish evil by destroying human freedom. God could seize a note, but He would not seize a man. Instead of conscripting man, God willed to consult humanity again as to whether or not it wanted to be made a member of the Divine orchestra once more. Almighty God, having given freedom to man, will not take it away again.

There was a Divine consultation with humanity, in which a Woman was asked by God if she would give Him human nature—"Will you freely give Me a new note out of humanity with which I can compose a new symphony?" In the name of all humanity, she consented: "Be it done unto Me." This new man must *be* a man; otherwise God would not be acting in the name of humanity. But he must also be outside the current of infection to which all men are subject. Being born of a Woman, He will be a man; being born of a Virgin, He will be a sinless man.

His Mother Mary then became to a new humanity what a lock is to a canal. If a ship is sailing on a polluted canal and wishes to transfer itself to clear waters on a higher level, it must pass through a device which locks out the polluted waters and raises the ship to the higher position. Then the other gate of the lock is lifted, and the ship rides on the new, clear waters, taking none of the polluted waters with it.

When God took upon Himself the human nature and became Christ through the Virgin Mother, He was the first note in the new melody. It is up to our personal will freely to incorporate ourselves to Him by faith, thus adding another note and creating a new humanity. We appropriate this saving grace by a free act, repeating the words of the Woman: "Be it done unto me."

Humanity is thus divided into two groups, namely, the old humanity which is still governed by the flesh, and the new, regenerated humanity which is governed by the Spirit: the humanity of goodness, love of God, love of neighbor.

The area of indifference is narrowing. The world is rapidly dividing into opposite poles of good and evil. The good are beginning to be better, and the evil are becoming worse.

It is of the good we would speak. The American people, who in the past have had good aspirations, are beginning to deepen and intensify them; thus do they strengthen this land of ours for the greater conflict against the alien forces of evil.

But as time goes on, the struggle in the world should be seen not as political or economic but as a conflict between two great forces of good and evil. Such is the deeper meaning of all our international conflicts.

How long the struggle will last, we know not. Whether it will be bloody or unbloody, we know not. How many swords will have to be unsheathed, or whether any sword will have to be unsheathed, that we know not. There is only one thing that we do know, and that is—we have already won! Only the news has not yet leaked out.

## CHAPTER TWENTY-THREE

# Fatigue

Do you wake up in the morning tired and exhausted? Do you have a heavy feeling and a dark brown taste in your mouth and feel run down at the heels? Then a word about fatigue.

It was at the close of the day, and two women were coming home on a bus after a shopping tour. One said to the other, "My feet are killing me."

The other one said, "You know, my feet never bother me as long as I have money in my pocketbook."

The fatigue which concerns us presently is not physical fatigue, but rather mental fatigue. Why is there so much apathy and dullness and indifference in the world, and such a want of fire and enthusiasm? Why do so many say of life, "I can't stand it any longer; it's too much for me?"

There are two explanations. One is the mechanical theory which holds that everyone has a definite amount of energy, which is limited. Fatigue follows from too lavish an expenditure. Energy is very much like having money in the bank. If you draw too many checks on it, you become exhausted.

Each person has a reservoir of energy which can be dissipated in a thousand channels. All fatigue on this theory is due to *exhaustion.*

The other theory might be called the "human" theory. It holds that if energy fails, it is not because the supply is used up, but because the channel is blocked, or because we did not use it properly. The chief cause of fatigue is not *exhaustion,* but *stagnation.* We are tired first in the mind, then in the body. Often it is the mind that makes the body tired. This demands an explanation of how the mind works.

The mind has two faculties. One faculty is the intellect, and the other faculty is the will. The faculty of intellect is for knowing; the faculty of the will is for choosing and doing. The object of the intellect is truth, and the object of the will is goodness or love. The will of itself is blind. The intellect or reason must lead the way. When the intellect presents a goal,

*e.g.*, visit London, the will pays it the compliment of wishfulness. Nothing is desired unless it is known. The intellect gives us the target, and the will shoots the arrow. It is one thing to know the goal and quite another thing to work toward it.

There are two general reasons why people are fatigued mentally. First, because they have no target; second, because they have too many targets.

By no target, we mean no philosophy of life. They would not have a gadget in the house for ten minutes without discovering its purpose, and yet they will live with themselves for ten, thirty, sixty years and not know why they are here or where they are going. Nothing so much creates boredom as the meaninglessness of life. If you give a boy a BB gun and a target, he is not so dangerous. If you give him a BB gun and no target, he is apt to shoot out the school window.

If you give people atomic bombs without a philosophy of life, you will start a world war. A boiler that has lost the purpose imposed upon it by an engineer is in danger of explosion. A society that has lost the goals and destiny imposed upon it by right reason and moral law becomes chaotic, revolutionary, and chilled with cold wars. Naturally, when minds lose the purpose of living, they lose the energy to work toward a goal. If a traveler loses interest in visiting Paris, the output of his energy in that direction declines.

Many, having lost the target of life, also lose interest in shooting arrows. This accounts for the tendency of many to deny they have freedom of will. Two of the most popular theories among the bored today are the Marxian and the Freudian. Marx holds that we are economically determined; Freud, that we are biologically determined. Despite all the talk about freedom today, the plain fact is that many are bored with freedom. That is why they are willing to surrender it to a dictator as Marxism demands or else are willing to deny any personal responsibility as Freudianism suggests, by denying moral guilt. Minds are tired principally because they have lost the pattern of life and, therefore, find it no longer worth living; or else, because seeing no purpose, they can see no reason for spending energy to save themselves from blind fatalism and deep, cavernous despair.

There is no danger of our universities and colleges losing academic freedom because professors are asked, "Are you a loyal, true American?" But there is grave danger that academic freedom may be lost by teachers saying that the students under them are not free; that they are determined economically, biologically, or socially. Give the students a target in life, a real goal, and then let them exercise their freedom toward that goal, and they will not suffer from the boredom of life.

A second reason for fatigue can be too many targets. People are unable to determine for themselves any fixed philosophy of life. One year they are reactionaries, with their feet firmly planted in cement. The next year they are liberals, with their feet firmly planted in mid-air. They read a best seller and for a month are idealists. Next month they read a book on materialism, and they become materialists. Suppose you got on a train with your mind made up to go to Chicago, and got off after an hour, and decided to go to New Orleans. Then you traveled one hundred miles and changed your mind, saying, "No, I will go to San Francisco." You traveled another hundred miles and said, "No, I will go to Indianapolis." If you did this long enough, you would go crazy. One university drove pigs crazy that way. They put their food in a certain slot, and after the pigs learned to go to that slot, they changed the slot. This went on indefinitely, the pigs getting a terrible fall from wrong slots, until they went crazy. The poor pigs would never go crazy by themselves. But man could drive them crazy by perverting their instincts and habits.

Something like that is happening to human beings. They are fatigued and exhausted from want of a permanent, over-all purpose in life. Can you imagine basketball players enjoying a game if the basket moved from one side of the gymnasium to the other whenever they took a shot? Minds are bored, worried, exhausted, and burdened with ennui because life is purposeless. If there is no meaning to life, there is not much use in living.

There are three ways to achieve power and to overcome fatigue:

1. Have a master idea.
2. Strengthen the will.
3. Have recourse to outside power.

*A master idea.* The mind is strengthened by a strong idea. An English professor of psychiatry tested weight lifters. The three men averaged lifting 101 pounds. He hypnotized them and told them they were strong. They lifted 142 pounds, or almost half more weight. Because they got the idea of strength, they became strong. He hypnotized them again and told them that they were weak. They lifted only 29 pounds. The idea of weakness induced weakness in action. The mind was exhausted before the body. At the time of the San Francisco earthquake, 30 people who had been in bed for 30 years got up and walked. The idea that they had to do something about their condition produced appropriate action.

The night before her wedding, the bride has in her mind one great "master idea," which need not be elaborated. The night before her wedding she stays up until two o'clock arranging her gown. She goes to bed and is up at four, not the least bit tired. Her idea of marriage gives her strength. But though she is up at four o'clock and starts dressing for the wedding, which is at eleven o'clock, she is invariably thirty-two minutes late for the church service. One year later, she has to get up to prepare seven o'clock breakfast for her husband, and she is exhausted; she has lost her master idea.

The ideomotor theory of psychology means that an idea tends to work itself out in action. You watch a football game from the stands. You can see an opening for the ball carried around right end. You instinctively move your body in that direction, simply because the idea prompted it. Get wrong ideas in your head and they come out as bad actions. It is nonsense to say that it does not make any difference what you think or believe, it all depends on how you act. If you think about robbing a bank, you will end up robbing one. Keep the mind clean and the body will keep clean.

The first master idea to possess is to realize we were made for happiness. But in order to be happy, we have to satisfy the higher part of our being, namely, our intellect and our will. We strive for Perfect Truth and Perfect Love, Which is God. The master idea then is that we are made to know, love, and serve God in this life and be happy with Him forever in the next. The body then becomes the servant of the mind, the senses minister to reason, and reason to faith. No one who loves this master idea is ever unhappy, even amidst the trials and vicissitudes of life. Energy multiplies to achieve it, by goodness to neighbors, patience, charity, meekness, resignation, and some of the other forgotten virtues, like courtesy and sacrifice. Life becomes full of zeal, and even though sometimes one may do wrong, one nevertheless always has the map. There are many people who get off the road and stay off because they have no road map. As long as you have a master idea, you can get back. There are two classes of people in the world: those who fall down and those who stay down. A pig falls in the mud and stays in the mud: a lamb falls in the mud and gets out of the mud.

Strong reasons make strong actions. To occupy yourself with love of God and neighbor is never to be idle. Hell is full of the talented, but Heaven, of the energetic. As sanctity declines, energy declines. Many today do not *believe* enough to be great. Mediocrity is the penalty for loss of faith.

*Strengthen the will.* Hardly ever does an educator today speak of training the will. A little boy asked his mother, "May I have another piece of cake?"

The mother said, "You have already had eight pieces."

"I know, Mother, but just let me have one more piece, please, please, please."

And the mother said, "All right."

Then the little boy said, "You haven't any will power at all, have you?"

There is a world of difference between willing and wanting. Most people *want* to be good, but they do not *will* to be good. Augustine said, before he became a saint, "Dear Lord, I want to be pure; not now, but a little later on." That was before he became a saint!

Many an alcoholic *wants* to be better; few *will* to be better. It is unfortunate today that some regard alcoholism as a disease like cancer. It may end as a disease, but it begins with an act of the will, namely, to take a drink. The repeated acts of the will become a habit, and the habit becomes enslavement. But even then there is left a little beachhead of human will that one can lay hold of and enlarge until the person is rehabilitated.

If people are told that they are animals or machines, they lose the sense of inner power to become better. A man is a slave of bad habit as long as he accepts the slavery. Why is it that those who constantly warn us of the danger of repressing our sex instincts never warn us about the danger of repressing our will to be better?

Character is like chiseling a statue; one has to knock off huge hunks of selfishness, which requires self-discipline. Only then does character begin to emerge. We mistakenly believe everything can be acquired without effort: for example, "How to learn French without studying vocabulary," or "How to learn to play the piano without reading notes," or "How to make money without working."

We never receive our second wind until we use up the first. God does not give us new graces until we exhaust ourselves in spending those already received. The condition of receiving new power is the resolute will to give power to others. We try to escape intellectual effort by reading picture magazines and novels exclusively and discover in the end that our power to think clearly has been lost. As George Bernard Shaw once said, "Our language is the language of Shakespeare, Thompson, and Milton, as we sit and croon like bilious pigeons."

Maybe our refusal to exercise our body could atrophy our muscles. Could the great increase of heart trouble be due to the fact that few exercise their hearts by hard exercise? I wonder if a ditchdigger ever developed angina pectoris? Maybe it is good for us that at our office and home we have to climb four flights of stairs for every meal.

Power is bought only in terms of willed service. Nonexpression of the will in effort and self-discipline has caused far more ravages than self-expression.

*Recourse to outside power*. The exercise of the will is right, but it is wrong if we think that we can do everything by our own will. We cannot lift ourselves by our own bootstraps or by the lobes of our ears. Those who rely only on their will generally become aggressive, domineering, self-willed, dictatorial, and proud. Human will has to depend on something else. The basic trouble with atheism is that it breathes the same air in that it breathes out.

There has to be another source of power outside our will. We do not nourish ourselves; we are dependent upon the plant and animal world outside. No organism is self-contained; it thrives only by contact with an environment which is non-self. We need air for our lungs and light for our eyes. When we are born, our mind is like our blackboard, on which nothing is written. Our five senses pour into the mind raw material, from which our intellect, like a great X ray, abstracts ideas, which we combine into judgments and reasoning processes.

Our spirits, too, are continuous with a larger spiritual world. We are not cisterns, but wells; we grow less by our own power than by assimilation of outside forces. Our intellect and will both need to cooperate with this Power of God. Once it gets into our intellect, it becomes faith; in our will, it becomes power. Divine Energy of Truth and Love does not originate in us but flows through us. As we establish contact with the atmosphere, which cannot be seen or tasted by breathing, so we establish commerce with the Divine Source of Power by prayer and the sevenfold channels which the Good Lord Himself offers to our depleted human forces. Unite a dedicated will with this Divine Energy and a character is transformed into inner peace and outer service. "I can do all things in Him Who strengtheneth Me."

Unfortunately, many have lost fire and enthusiasm. What has become of great patriots; of an intense devotion and love of country? A country is strong when it has faith in right; it is weak when it loses faith. Only a restoration of our firm belief in God will shake off indifference and apathy and a sense of opiate that makes us cold to international injustices.

Communism is a "faith," a "philosophy of life" based on hate and confiscation. Communism can be overcome only by another faith, a faith in God, a faith in His Moral Law, and a faith in the Providential destiny of our country.

It behooves all of us to take pride in the words that Washington spoke at Valley Forge: "Put only Americans on guard tonight."

CHAPTER TWENTY-FOUR

# Peace Tactics of the Soviets

Ever since the day the angels sang the hymns of peace over the hills of Bethlehem, all men have wanted peace. No people on the face of the earth really want it more than the American people. But we can be victims of "false peace." Ruskin has warned us that peace may be either *bought* or it may be *won.* It is won by resistance to evil; it is bought by compromise with evil.

In this hour, when we are hearing so very much of peace, it behooves us to ask ourselves, "What is peace?"

There are three different definitions of peace:

1. The Communist notion of peace.
2. The bourgeois notion of peace.
3. The true concept of peace.

The Communist notion of peace is both a *tactic* and a *goal.* For no other people on earth is peace both a tactic and a goal as it is for the Reds. In this duality of purpose lies their trickery.

Peace as a *tactic* means the use of nonviolent and nonmilitary methods in order to prepare for violent offense and the demoralization of other nations. The *goal* of Communist peace is the complete subservience of the world to Communist dictatorship. For the Communists there can be no real peace until there has been a complete destruction of all private property, the abolition of morals and religion, the subjection of all democratic processes to a totalitarian dictator. That is the goal; but the tactic is to talk peace in order to induce nations to disarm and to convince them that the Moscow-inspired revolutions are purely local. By these ruses they hope to demoralize the rest of the world and prepare for its ultimate conquest.

The bourgeois concept of peace is a negative idea, namely, peace is the absence of war. There are many who would settle for that kind of peace. Very often it is purchased at the cost of justice, and even at the cost of liberty and right. Such "peace" often brings a cold war in which everybody is in hot water. Peace is not the absence of war, as a diamond is not the absence of carbon. Peace must have some positive concept, which brings us to the true concept of peace.

The true definition of peace is: Peace is the tranquillity of order—not tranquillity alone, because robbers can be tranquil in the possession of their spoils. The sea is tranquil very often before a storm. Peace is the tranquillity of order, and order implies justice, and justice implies law. There is peace in an individual when there is subordination of senses to reason, of reason to faith, of body to soul, of the whole personality to God.

Peace is inseparable from justice. One does not really set out to have peace; peace is a by-product of justice. *Pax opus justitiae:* "Peace is the work of justice." There is national and international peace when everyone is rendering to his neighbor that which is his due, when citizens recognize and honor God, the Supreme Lawgiver, and when each nation agrees that all other peoples and other nations should share in the economic blessings of the earth.

It is important to decide which of these three concepts we will adopt. It should not be too embarrassing to choose. A tramp came to a farmer one day and asked for a little work. The farmer said, "You go down to the basement. There you will find a number of potatoes. I want you to put them into three piles. Put all of the good ones in one pile, all of the bad ones in another pile, and then in the middle, you can put those that are just half good and half bad."

About an hour later the tramp said to the farmer, "I don't want the job. It drives me crazy making decisions."

There is no escaping a decision about peace, and it must be the right one. It may be helpful to inquire how we fool ourselves, how we have been fooled, and how Russia has fooled us.

We fool ourselves by failing to make a proper distinction between the philosophy of Communism and Russian foreign policy. Many Americans were deceived in the past fifteen years because they judged the Soviets by their foreign policy rather than by their philosophy. The foreign policy of Russia is only a tactic, a maneuver, a scheme, a strategy, and an imposture.

When Soviet Russia's foreign policy was favorable to the United States and to the Western powers, many believed Russia's Communism was good. When Soviet Russia's foreign policy was unfavorable to the Western powers, they believed Communism was bad. If we judged Russia by its philosophy, Soviet foreign policy would never deceive us. We would know that its philosophy is intrinsically wicked and is bent on the subjugation of mankind to dictatorship, even when its foreign policy for a moment is coincidental with our own.

A burglar enters a jewelry store with a philosophy of life, which is to gain his livelihood by stealing. His first trip into the store is to "case the joint." That is his foreign policy; he looks at a few jewels, may even put down a deposit on a small gem. A short time later the jeweler finds that he has been robbed. We can lose our freedom in exactly the same way, unless we realize that Soviet Russia in the United Nations and the United States is "casing the world." Be warned against the robbery of our heritage of freedom.

The new tactic of the Soviets is to convince us that "Russia is no longer the same. There is a new dictator; his name is Malenkov. He wishes to dwell in peace with the world." Incidentally, his name in Russian means "insignificant." The press tells us Malenkov is going to be "much more favorable to the Western powers; Stalin was not. If Malenkov makes an overture of peace, we should accept it." Let us not be fooled. Keep in mind the distinction between the philosophy of Communism and the tactics. If Malenkov subscribes to the philosophy of Communism, he is bent on world destruction.

Coming back to the example of the jeweler who was robbed once. He remembered the burglar who came in; he looked like

Stalin. So the jeweler said, "I am not going to be deceived again." Another crook came in, this time rather a nice-looking crook. The jeweler said, "Oh, well, he doesn't belong to a gang. This is a fine-looking fellow. He wears spats and has a cane." That could be Malenkov.

If the jeweler is smart, he will ask himself, not how a man looks, not how he appears; he will ask himself, "Does he believe in the philosophy of stealing?" If he knows the visitor believes in the philosophy of stealing, he will not be deceived again.

We Americans have a very short memory. Let us go back and recall how we were deceived before. Remember how this country swallowed Communism from 1936 until 1939. After the signing of the Nazi-Soviet treaty there was an interlude of common sense. When the Nazis and the Soviets broke, many went overboard for Russia. Read the editorials in newspapers from 1942 to 1945, and you will be amazed to see how many supported Russia and Communism. In those days one member of the State Department who could not speak Russian but who had learned the Communist *Internationale* by heart, sang it at midnight before Lincoln's memorial statue in Washington.

In those days it was unsafe for anyone to say anything against Soviet Russia or Communism. I know. What stories we could tell of abuse and slander because of a warning to the American people that Russia intended to take over all of Eastern Europe after the war. For daring to say such things one was accused of being antidemocratic, for in those days

Russia was praised as "one of the great democracies of the world." But no one was deceived in those days who judged Soviet Russia by its philosophy.

I remember in preparation for an Easter broadcast writing into the text, "Poland was crucified by two thieves; the two thieves being the Nazis and the Soviets." I received a telegram from one of my censors telling me that I would not be permitted to say that over the radio. I sent the censor a telegram saying, "Would it be all right to call Russia the good thief?" He did not think it a bit funny.

In those days Communists were worming their way into schools, universities, government, and offices of columnists. During those days of the honeymoon with Russia, I was going into my class at the Catholic University in Washington. A very clean-cut, fine-looking man with steel gray eyes met me at the door and said, "I have something very important to tell you."

"It is now class time; if you wish to come in, you may sit down for the hour. Otherwise, kindy wait, and I will see you afterward."

He attended the class, and at the end he said, "I was very interested in this lecture. I am an escaped Russian. Here is the story of my life." He gave me a book, saying, "I want you to read it and then get in touch with me." He gave me his name, address, and telephone number. I said, "I may not have time to read it; would you tell me what is important in the book?"

So we thumbed it through together. He belonged to a rather large family, some of whom were killed in the Bolshevik Revolution. He joined the Communist party and for a time, because of some minor disobedience, was sentenced to Siberia. Upon his release, he joined the Russian Merchant Marine. He said he had the intent to escape, and one night he jumped ship. He was much farther from shore than he had believed and was in danger of sinking. He said that he prayed to the Person of Our Lord and was saved. The book ended with these words: "From now on, I dedicate myself to the cause of God and America."

I asked, "Where do I come in?"

"Well," he said, "I want to help you. I know about your lectures on Communism, all you have written about it, and I would like to travel with you when you lecture. Just let me talk ten minutes after you, and tell the people my first-hand information about this terrible tyranny of Communism, and how I have suffered under it. I have Communist documents which I have brought with me from Russia. These documents I will translate for you. I have even some inside information on the Secret Police and on Stalin, and all this will help you in your lectures. Now that I have found refuge in America, will you please let me help you in this battle against Communism?"

I said, "I will let you know in forty-eight hours."

He said, "Can you let me know in twenty-four?"

"Yes, maybe I can."

As soon as he left, I called up the F.B.I. and said, "I have a Soviet agent who has just visited me, and this is his name. Will you look up his record?"

Half an hour later, the F.B.I. called me up and said, "Yes,

he is one of their most dangerous agents. We had traced him to Manchuria, then to China, and then into the Philippines. We did not know he was in the United States. That particular book was printed in Russia to deceive you; your life could be in danger. Give us his address and telephone number, and we will take over."

The insinuation of Communists into American institutions by peaceful tactics were merely putting into practice the Communist theory of peace. Communism took over Russia, Stalin explained, by using peace tactics. In *Problems of Leninism*, Stalin said, "We used the mighty weapon of peace. It created mass sympathy for our revolution, both in the West among the workers and in the East among oppressed people."

The Sixth World Congress in 1928 gave these orders to the Communists throughout the world: "Accelerate the deterioration of home morale through the lavish use of *peace slogans* and thus prepare for insurrection."

Lange, in his famous book *The Road to Victory*, which is still used as a textbook in Russia, gave this motto to Communism: *Si vis bellum, garri pacem*—"If you want to begin a war, talk peace, use peace slogans."

As Lenin himself said, "It is necessary to use every cunning unlawful method, evasion and concealment of the truth for the sake of the revolution." Stalin in his *Problems of Leninism* told us what Communist dictatorship was like. "Dictatorship means nothing more nor less than the power which rests directly *on violence, which is not limited by any laws, or restricted by any absolute rules*."

Fellow citizens, be not deceived. Remember, when Russia talks peace, it is a tactic, and a preparation for war. Russia says it wants peace. The peace it wants is a piece of China, a piece of Hungary, a piece of Poland. A peace overture of Russia will be the beginning of another Pearl Harbor.

If true peace is to be won, it must first be won in our own hearts. Let us turn back to God and establish justice in our souls. Russia will perish because it is anti-God; but we shall not survive if in the face of Communism we are Godless. If we put ourselves on God's side, then who shall be against us? May God keep our minds clear and our hearts pure, that we may never be deceived by the false peace of the Soviets. As Dante put it, "In Thy Will, God, is our peace."

CHAPTER TWENTY-FIVE

# Reparation

Our little angel has just received an "angelgram" from Heaven. He was told that next Tuesday night he has to report back in Heaven. Since we cannot go on without our angel, we shall have only one more telecast this season.

Our last subject was peace from a negative point of view. We warned that Russia uses peace talk as a tactic and that the danger of war increases with each overture of peace from the Soviets. Russia is very much like a man rowing a boat. He rows one way and looks another. Goethe well said, "We are never deceived; we deceive ourselves."

Here we are concerned with peace from a positive point of view, namely, how it is achieved in the individual and in the nation. Lincoln's testimony will be invoked as pointing out the national condition for peace. It may take some time to get to Lincoln, in which case we shall be like a lawyer who was arguing at great length before the judge, presenting one precedent after another. He felt that he was getting a little too deep and confusing for the judge; so he inquired of the judge, "Your Honor, are you following me?"

The judge said, "I follow you all right, but if I knew the way back, I would leave you now."

Suffering is related to guilt in a general way, though each individual who suffers is not individually guilty. World suffering and world crisis are also related to guilt and guilt needs reparations, or the righting of wrong.

Our modern world very seldom thinks of the relationship of a world crisis to guilt. The modern world practically ignores guilt as responsibility for the violation of a moral law. A man who disobeys one of God's physical laws, for example, that he should eat to live, after four or five days suffers a headache. It is just as vain to deny that the breaking of moral laws has consequences as to deny that the breaking of physical laws produces certain effects. Unfortunately, many live amidst crises, trials, cold wars, and political disorders without any sense of guilt. They fail to see a connection between what is happening in the world order and the way we live, think, and move. This denial of responsibility reminds us of a husband and wife who went to the doctor. The doctor asked the husband, "What is wrong with you, sir?"

He said, "I eat too many cherries."

The wife said, "At the bottom of cocktail glasses."

As he blamed the sickness on cherries and not on alcohol, so too many in our modern world forget that perhaps our world headache may be due to the way we have conducted ourselves before our fellow man and before God, rather than to our political cherries.

An analogy is to be found among the egotists and the selfish, whom nobody seems to like. Failing to see that their egotism has alienated their neighbor, they accuse their neighbor of being antisocial. Instead of looking into their own hearts, they disclaim responsibility for their self-centeredness and place the blame, perhaps, on halitosis. They try using chlorophyl for thirty days, but they still are unpopular. They never shoulder the guilt of egotism, which alone would lead to a more generous attitude to others. Of such people it has been said, "They have no enemies; all their friends hate them."

Nations, too, can get in the habit of denying that their trials, the hatred of other nations, their insecurity, and the threat of Communism may be related to their moral failings. It is too superficial a justification for any nation to blame another for its crises.

Granted now that nations as well as individuals can violate God's laws, it follows that the evil that brings us to the tragic predicament must be expiated. Greek drama and all the great philosophies of the East and West are full of the idea that guilt must be atoned for. There is no British God, no American God. God is the Father of all men, and His Lordship is exercised over all history. God's Will and man's will are interlocked in every heart and in every nation. When man's will rebels against God's Will, man creates a tragic situation, which in the person is a sense of guilt, and in the community of nations, a crisis. Our tragedy today is due basically to the human will opposing the Divine Will.

The next point is: Guilt needs reparation. There is a great difference between sorrow for the wrong we did and making reparation for it. Suppose that during one of these telecasts, when my little angel came out to clean my blackboard, I stole his halo. I am sure that when my little angel took himself back into the wings, if I said, "I am awfully sorry, little angel; will

you forgive me?" the angel would answer, "Sure I forgive you!" But he would say, "Give me back my halo." The return of the halo would be the proof that I was sorry for the theft.

Suppose every time we did wrong we were told to drive a nail in a board; and every time we were forgiven we were told to pull a nail out. The board would be full of holes. These holes are the record of how our wrong deeds disturb the order of justice. Many think that all they have to do when they do wrong individually or socially is merely to ask to be forgiven. They must also make reparation for the wrong. The equilibrium and the balance of justice have been disturbed, and that balance must be restored by penance.

Suppose you had the moral authority to command and bind me in conscience. Presently I am on neutral ground, just like the neutral in the old gearshift. You tell me to take three steps to the right. But, being very "self-expressive," I take three to the left. When I find myself in a place which does not give me happiness, I say to you, "I am sorry; will you forgive me?"

You will forgive me; but look where I am. Before I can begin doing good, I have to get back in neutral again. If I put my foot three times down in self-affirmation or in an unlawful pleasure, I have to put my foot down three times in reparation; it is rather humiliating, but I put my little tail behind my legs and get back to neutral. Then I can begin to move to the right and the thing that gives me peace of soul.

A nation may do wrong; if so, it must make up for it by some kind of penance and atonement and reparation. We can do wrong as a nation; we are not all white, innocent lambs. While it may be true that other nations have done far greater wrong, the way to peace is not to point out their villainy. Rather it is humbly to admit our failures and make expiation for them. Can we wash our hands Pilate-like of guilt for China, Poland, and the countries behind the Iron Curtain and Bamboo Curtain? We are responsible to some extent for the slavery forced upon these lands. It is not honest to lay all the blame on Communism. Part of the tragedy is due to our own unfulfilled moral duties. As American people, we should affirm before God and the world that the crisis is partly of our own making;

the world is the way it is, because you are the way you are, and I am the way I am.

It is not sufficient that we as individuals make up for our own individual failings. We are also citizens of a great republic, and we have to make the expiation as a republic. This will involve some prayers and penances on our part. It will also mean seeing that as long as human groups do not make sacrifices for peace, they will continue to settle their difficulties by war. War to egotists who deny they ever do wrong seems a smaller calamity than the renunciation of their egotism and selfishness.

National penance is a true American doctrine, as well as a profound religious doctrine in the great Hebraic-Christian tradition. Lincoln expressed this better than any President our glorious country has ever had. Maybe he knew it because he was better schooled in sacrifice and suffering. Lincoln had about completed his first term as President and there were many who opposed his reelection. Shortly before the next election a meeting was held in New York. Present among others were Stephen T. Field, whom Lincoln had appointed to the Supreme Court; Roscoe Conkling, Speaker of the House; Whitelaw Reid; and Horace Greeley. They all agreed that everything possible should be done to prevent the renomination of Lincoln.

It was then that Orville Browning, a friend of Lincoln, wrote, "I thought that Lincoln might get through the Presidency, as many a boy gets through college, without disgrace and without knowledge; but I fear he is a total failure."

While the Civil War was raging, the knifing of Lincoln continued. One paper accused Lincoln of drawing his salary in gold, while soldiers received theirs in depreciated greenbacks. It was a lie; Lincoln was taking his pay in salary warrants payable in greenbacks, which he did not cash generally until several months after he received them. Lincoln, hearing of this calumny, made an accounting of what he had. Lincoln pulled open the drawer of his desk, took out a few stocks, bankbooks, and deeds for some real estate, and, carrying it in his big, long arms, he walked from the White House over to the Treasury. Coming to the desk of Mr. Chase, the Secretary of the Treasury, Lincoln said, "Here are all my earthly possessions. Put them all in government bonds, for the sake of the country."

One night while the enemy barked at Lincoln, he took a sheet of paper and wrote, "It will be my duty to so cooperate with the President-elect so as to save the Union between the election and the inauguration." He signed his name and put it back into his desk.

Lincoln ran for a second term. As the returns came in, a friend told him that one of his political enemies in Maryland was being defeated. Lincoln said, "You have more personal resentment than I. Perhaps I have too little of it, but I never thought it paid. A man has no time to spend half his life in quarrels. If a man ceases to attack me, I never hold the past against him."

At two thirty on election night, as the telegraphic reports

came into the White House, Lincoln stayed up to read them. The band was playing outside. Lincoln began to reminisce to his friends about an incident after the first election. He came home exhausted, looked into a mirror on the other side of the room, and saw in the mirror two faces—one his own image, which was very clear; but behind it was another image of him that was quite shadowy. Not knowing what it meant, he got up, walked around the room, and looked again. The two images appeared—one clear and the other ghostly. He asked Mary, his wife, what it meant; she said, "It means you will be elected two terms. The first one you will live through, and before the second one is finished, you will die."

Out of this life of sorrow, misjudgment, trial, and war, a great character was made. His Calvaries enabled him to have an insight into the spiritual needs of a nation that is given to but a few. On the cold, windy day of his second inaugural, he asked the American people to make some kind of reparation for their national sins:

> It is the duty of nations as well as of men to own their dependence upon the overruling Power of God; to confess their sins and transgressions in humble sorrow, yet with assured hope that genuine repentance will lead to mercy and pardon; and to recognize the sublime Truth announced in the Holy Scriptures and proven by all history, that these nations only are blessed.
>
> And inasmuch as we know that by His Divine Law, nations, like individuals, are subjected to punishments and chastisements in this world, may we not justly fear that the awful calamity of Civil

War which now desolates the land may be but a punishment inflicted upon us for our presumptuous sins, to the needful end of our national reformation as a whole people? We have been the recipients of the choicest bounties of Heaven. We have been preserved these many years in peace and prosperity. We have grown in numbers, wealth and power as no other nation has ever grown; but we have forgotten God. We have forgotten the Gracious Hand that preserved us in peace, and multiplied and enriched and strengthened us; and we have vainly imagined, in the deceitfulness of our hearts, that all these blessings were produced by some superior virtue and wisdom of our own. Intoxicated with unbroken success, we have become too self-sufficient to feel the necessity of redeeming and preserving Grace, too proud to pray to the God that made us.

It behooves us then, to humble ourselves before the Offended Power, to confess our national sins, and to pray for clemency and forgiveness.

Lincoln clearly taught that the awful calamity of Civil War was the punishment that God permitted us to have because of our national sins. Would it not be well to let ring through America today a voice like Lincoln's, summoning us to fall prostrate before God and ask God for pardon and forgiveness. We need not go to war, thus destroying our fellow man and turning poppy fields into rivers of blood. There is another way of peace, and we believe our President can lead us down that road. In his inaugural address he did not think of God as an afterthought. He began it by invoking the blessing of God. Given this consciousness of Divine protection, would it not be well to write or telegraph, asking our President to declare a National Day of Prayer and Penance? [1]

The Communists are not the only ones who are guilty before God. We, too, as a nation are guilty. We have failed in some way. As Lincoln said:

> It behooves us then, to humble ourselves before the Offended Power, to confess our national sins, and to pray for clemency and forgiveness.

[1] On June 23, 1953, President Eisenhower issued this proclamation:

BY THE PRESIDENT OF THE UNITED STATES OF AMERICA

A PROCLAMATION

WHEREAS, at the very beginning of our national existence, the signers of the Declaration of Independence invoked "the protection of divine Providence" with faith and with humility; and

WHEREAS, since then, we as a Nation have been wont to turn to Almighty God for guidance and strength, especially in times of national stress; and

WHEREAS, in the words of Abraham Lincoln, penned on one such occasion in the year 1863, "it is the duty of nations as well as of men to own their dependence upon the overruling power of God, to confess their sins and transgressions in humble sorrow, yet with assured hope that genuine repentance will lead to mercy and pardon"; and

WHEREAS, in recognition of our continuing need for divine aid, the Congress, by a joint resolution approved on April 17, 1952, 66 Stat. 64, provided that the President should set aside and proclaim a suitable day each year, other than a Sunday, as a National Day of Prayer, on which the people of the United States may turn to God in prayer and meditation:

NOW, THEREFORE, I, DWIGHT D. EISENHOWER, President of the United States of America, do hereby designate Saturday, July 4, 1953—the one hundred and seventy-seventh anniversay of the adoption of the Declaration of Independence in firm reliance on God's transcendent power—as a National Day of Penance and Prayer; and I request all of our people to turn to Him in humble supplication on that day, in their homes or in their respective places of worship. With contrite hearts, let us pray for God's help in solving the grave problems which confront us, and render thanks to Him for watching over our Nation throughout its history.

IN WITNESS WHEREOF, I have hereunto set my hand and caused the Seal of the United States of America to be affixed.

DONE at the City of Washington this twenty-third day of June in the year of our Lord nineteen hundred and fifty-three, and of the Independence of the United States of America the one hundred and seventy-seventh.

(SEAL)

DWIGHT D. EISENHOWER

## CHAPTER TWENTY-SIX

# The Role of Communism and the Role of America

The world is sick, not just one part of the world. When a human organism is poisoned, one cannot amputate an arm or a leg, thus completely eradicating the infection. Neither is any one nation in the world wholly to blame for the crisis—not even Russia. We have all sinned, and all stand in need of the Mercy of God.

What is the role of Communism? The best answer is in the words of Our Divine Lord, "Where the body is, there shall the eagles be gathered together."

When an animal or a human dies in the desert, for the moment one can see nothing in the clear sky; but suddenly from out of the mountain fastnesses and rocky crags, great vultures of the skies come down to this glittering rottenness to devour it. Let corruption begin, and these winged monsters appear, shrieking and croaking, at their banquet of death. They are avengers as well as scavengers: a judgment on death and corruption. But they may also be Providential, for what diseases and pestilences might ravage mankind if these vultures were not there to consume rottenness!

Whenever a civilization begins to die, morally or spiritually, other vultures appear, and they are equally a judgment on corruption. Such is the mission of Communism in the world: to be the *scavenger of decaying civilization.* Once a culture begins to rot from the inside, there immediately appear outside, with boding voices, monsters gathering for the spoil. The vultures may even find their advance agents or fellow travelers within the civilization that begins to rot. Communism is playing, in our day, the role of a winged scavenger with mechanical wings of hammer and sickle, bringing judgment on those countries that have lost their faith in God and morals.

Arnold Toynbee asserts that 16 out of 19 civilizations that have decayed since the beginning of the world up to the present have decayed from within. Lincoln always said that America would never be conquered from without. If it ever perishes, and please God it will not, it will do so from within.

The proper way is to look upon Communism and see it as the judgment of God. As Assyria was the "rod and staff" of God in former times, so Soviet Russia is that scourge today. Think not that Communism is an invasion of an ideology completely alien to the Western world. Nor is it something of which the Western world can wash its hands, saying, "Behold, I am innocent of the blood of this Red Thing."

Communism came out of our Western civilization; it was produced out of what was putrid, foul, and rotten in the atheism and materialism of the nineteenth century. There is not a single philosophical idea in Communism that did not come from the West. Marx, who was a German, put together the dialectics of Hegel, which he studied in Berlin, and the materialism of Feuerbach, which he read about later. Afterwards, he added sociology learned from Proudhon in France and some bad economics gleaned from his readings in the British Museum. Marx never thought Russia would be the first country to adopt Communism. On his principles, it should have been the last. But what Russia did add to Communism was the power, the dynamism, the despotism, and the cruelty of an Asiatic soul.

When, then, the Soviets communize Eastern Europe and win supporters through Western Europe, let it be remembered that it is merely bringing back what it once got. If Europe and America are scandalized at Communism, it is merely because the Soviets are wholesaling what Western civilization once retailed. Communism makes inroads because of the vacuum created in the Western world through its loss of faith in God. One need only notice the type of soul to which Communism appeals in our own civilization, and one finds a suggestion of the type of civilization to which it will appeal. Healthy bodies can counteract germs; weak bodies cannot. Communism is *active* barbarism from without, but it can make progress only when there is *passive* barbarism from within. Steel needs moisture to become rusty; civilization needs damp brains to become communized.

If we see Communism then as a judgment on ourselves, we shall be more humble before God and better equipped to resist it. It is at one and the same time an *effect* and also a *judgment* on our Western world. Communism has its role to play. Communism is not garbage; it is manure, a fertilizer. A death is spread on the world in this our winter of discontent, unconsciously preparing the new life of a better springtime, when the world finally finds its way back again to God. Communism will never be destroyed by war; it will be *converted;* evil can be overcome only by good.

When Russia does receive the gift of faith, its role will be that of an apostle to the rest of the world. It will help bring faith to the rest of the world. Why are we so hopeful about Russia? Why should it be the means of evangelizing nations of the earth? Because Russia has fire; Russia has zeal. God could do something with the hate of a Saul, by turning it into love. He could do something with the passion of a Magdalen, by converting it to zeal; but God can do nothing with those who are neither hot nor cold. These He will vomit from His Mouth.

The great shame of our world is that we have the truth, but we have no zeal. Communists have zeal, but they have no truth. Communism is like a fire that is spreading itself all over the world; it is almost an inverted Pentecost. Someday, instead of turning downward, that fire will begin to burn upward and in true Pentecostal fashion, bringing life and peace and joy to men instead of hate, destruction, and death.

Our Western world lacks that fire. There are no longer any deep loves or passionate devotion to great causes; expediency and self-interest are too general. Politics and economics are our major interests, and neither can warm the souls of men.

Our fires of patriotism, evangelization, and zeal are being reduced to embers. We are cold, dull, and apathetic. One tiny effect of that want of fire is the fact that in our Western world there are but few orators. Most men in public life are readers. They are so little possessed of a love of great truths that their lips have no burning overflow. What young woman would ever take a man as a husband who wrote out a wedding proposal? Glory be to God, if He loves the woman, he ought to be able to talk about it! If we love God, we ought to be able to talk about Him. If we love our country, we ought to be able to talk about our country. If we love our sciences, we ought to be able to talk about our sciences.

Did the English Episcopalian minister, G. Studdert Kennedy, correctly describe the situation in his poem "Indifference," written during World War I, in which he contrasted Our Lord coming to Calvary and coming to the modern city of Birmingham?

When Jesus came to Golgotha,
They hanged Him on a tree,
They drove great nails through hands and feet,
And made a Calvary;
They crowned Him with a crown of thorns,
Red were His wounds and deep,
For those were crude and cruel days,
And human flesh was cheap.

When Jesus came to Birmingham
They simply passed Him by,
They never hurt a hair of Him,
They only let Him die;

For men had grown more tender,
  And they would not give Him pain,
They only just passed down the street
  And left Him in the rain.

Still Jesus cried, "Forgive them
  For they know not what they do,"
And still it rained the winter rain
  That drenched Him through and through;
The crowds went home and left the streets
  Without a soul to see
And Jesus crouched against a wall,
  And cried for Calvary.

The hate and violence on Calvary was more bearable to Christ than the broad-minded indifference of those who saw no God worth embracing, no evil worth condemning.

This Russian fire has tremendous potentialities. The Communists do not deny God; they merely challenge God. They are not like college sophomores who deny God because they have read the first ten pages of a biology textbook. The Soviets are militant; they are fighting against Him because they know He exists. Someday they will love Him. When they do, they will mediate between a reborn Europe and Asia, and, out of Russia, God will find His best Galilee to choose fishers of men for restoring true peace to the world.

What is the role of America? We are destined, under Providence, to be the secondary cause for the restoration of the freedom and liberties of the peoples of the world. We are the *secondary* cause; God is the *primary* cause. To fulfill that role, we shall have to make ourselves worthy of it.

Our country has always had a great mission. In the beginning of our history we were a sanctuary for the oppressed. In our times we became an arsenal for democracy. In the last few years we have been the pantry for the starving world. Each year we send millions of dollars to the distressed and hungry of the world. In the near future, we may be called upon to roll up the curtain of the Eastern world, that is, to give to the East the prosperity, peace, and fraternity with the other nations of the earth which it so ardently desires.

Our great country was hidden from the eyes of men for centuries behind a veil. The ships of Columbus pierced that veil and brought this vast continent into view. Now, it is the destiny of America to pierce another veil, the veil of the Eastern peoples of the world, in whom we are so interested in our missions. Our role is to restore these people to some decency of living. At present, two-thirds of the people of the world go to bed hungry every night. To fill their stomachs with our abundance and to fill their souls with the truth of God is our task and our mission.

To fulfill this role, we must make ourselves worthy. That involves sounding the mystery of Our Lord, Who said, "I came not to bring peace, but the sword."

Peter thought that He meant a sword that swings outward to kill others. The night Our Lord was arrested, Peter drew a sword, and as a swordsman he proved to be an excellent fisherman. The best he could do was hack off the ear of the servant of a high priest. The Lord reprimanded him: "Put the sword again into its scabbard. They who take the sword will perish by the sword."

Our Blessed Lord was telling Peter, "When I say 'I came to bring the sword,' I mean not a sword to thrust into the enemy, but a sword to thrust into yourself, to root out your selfishness and sin." This is the sword that brings peace.

America has a more beautiful destiny than it knows. If there is any way of telling what that destiny is, it might be likened to that of Simon of Cyrene, who was a stranger in the city on the day that Christ was crucified. He stationed himself on the roadway, to watch Our Lord go to His death. He did not know who He was, but he was curious, as some men are about other men going to death. As he watched the procession of the Son of God carrying His cross, the long arm of the Roman law reached out to him, commanding, "Take up His cross! Carry it!" He did not want to do it; but he took it and followed in the footsteps. Soon the yoke became sweet and the burden light.

America is at the crossroads, too—the crossroads of the suffering world. It sees the world being crucified by Communism. The long arm of Providence is reaching out to America, saying, "Take up thy cross! The cross of all the starving people of the world. Carry it!"

Our great country does not know whose cross it is carrying. Actually we are carrying a nobler cross than we know. We are bearing a nobler cross than we deserve. We have already saved the world from the swastika, which would cross out the cross and make a double cross. Now we must save the

world from the hammer and the sickle: the hammer that crucifies, and the sickle that cuts life like immature wheat that it may never be one with the Bread of Life.

America's role is to change these symbols so that one day the hammers carried aloft will look like crosses as they parade in the Name of God; and the sickle will look like the moon under the feet of the Lady to whom these telecasts are dedicated. May they help bring us to God and make Americans love one another, for the betterment of the world and the peace of the human soul.